ORIGINS OF THE WITCHES' SABBATH

MAGIC in HISTORY

SOURCEBOOKS SERIES

THE ARRAS WITCH TREATISES
Andrew Colin Gow, Robert B. Desjardins, and François V. Pageau

HAZARDS OF THE DARK ARTS:
Advice for Medieval Princes on Witchcraft and Magic
Richard Kieckhefer

The Magic in History Sourcebooks series features compilations and translations of key primary texts that illuminate specific aspects of the history of magic and the occult from within. Each title is tightly focused, but the scope of the series is chronologically and geographically broad, ranging from ancient to modern and with a global reach. Selections are in readable and reliable English, annotated where necessary, with brief contextualizing introductions.

SERIES EDITORS

RICHARD KIECKHEFER
Northwestern University

CLAIRE FANGER
Rice University

ORIGINS OF THE WITCHES' SABBATH

MICHAEL D. BAILEY

The Pennsylvania State University Press

University Park, Pennsylvania

Library of Congress
Cataloging-in-Publication Data

Names: Bailey, Michael David,
    1971– author.
Title: Origins of the witches'
    sabbath / Michael D. Bailey.
Other titles: Magic in history
    sourcebooks series.
Description: University Park,
    Pennsylvania : The Pennsylvania
    State University Press, [2021]
    | Series: Magic in history
    sourcebooks series | Includes
    bibliographical references and
    index.
Summary: "Explores the western
    European idea of the witches'
    sabbath, based on translations
    of five texts dating from the
    1430s, and examines how these
    texts went on to influence
    conceptions of diabolical
    witchcraft for centuries to
    come"—Provided by publisher.
Identifiers: LCCN 2020043414 |
    ISBN 9780271089102
    (paperback)
Subjects: LCSH: Sabbat—Alps,
    Western—History—To
    1500—Sources. | Witchcraft—
    Alps, Western—History—To
    1500—Sources.
Classification: LCC BF1572.
    S28 B35 2021 | DDC
    133.4/3093634—dc23
LC record available at https://lccn
    .loc.gov/2020043414

Published by The Pennsylvania State
University Press,
University Park, PA 16802–1003

The Pennsylvania State University
Press is a member of the Association
of University Presses.

It is the policy of The Pennsylvania
State University Press to use
acid-free paper. Publications on
uncoated stock satisfy the minimum
requirements of American National
Standard for Information Sciences—
Permanence of Paper for Printed
Library Material, ANSI Z39.48–1992.

CONTENTS

ACKNOWLEDGMENTS

First and foremost, I must thank Catherine Chène, Franck Mercier, Georg Modestin, Martine Ostorero, and Kathrin Utz Tremp, whose outstanding work on the original sources made these translations possible. My very first scholarly article dealt with several of these texts, and I have pondered putting them into English for a long time. For allowing me the opportunity, I thank Iowa State University, which granted me a year of leave under the auspices of a Faculty Professional Development Assignment. I was awarded the FPDA to work on a different project (which I did), but it also afforded time to begin these translations in earnest. I am also grateful to my colleague David Hollander, who cheerfully consulted with me on bits of curious Latin, and who generously created the map of the western Alps.

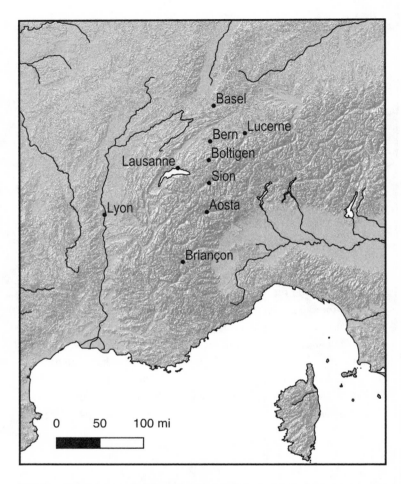

MAP Locations associated with witchcraft and witches' sabbaths in the western Alps. Courtesy of David Hollander.

General Introduction

The sources translated here depict a remarkable transformation. Most people in medieval Europe broadly accepted the reality of harmful magic, or *maleficium*, as it was most commonly termed in Latin.[1] Likewise they accepted that there were certain wicked people who practiced such magic. Labeled in various ways (masculine *malefici* or feminine *maleficae* were just some of the options), these "witches" were often imagined to be terrible figures. They might injure, rob, or even kill their neighbors, and they were generally thought to be involved in some way with dark forces, for Christianity taught that almost all magic ultimately stemmed from the devil.[2] They were not, however, typically believed to gather together as members of organized heretical sects or as agents of a vast diabolical conspiracy that aimed to undermine all of Christian society. That idea emerged only very late in the medieval era, crystalizing in a handful of texts written within the space of a single decade (the 1430s) and clustered geographically around the arc of the western Alps.

In Lucerne, the civic chronicler Hans Fründ penned a brief report on a series of witch trials in the neighboring region of Valais that had claimed the lives of more than one hundred people over the course of about a year and a half. Claude Tholosan was also a secular official, the chief magistrate of Briançon in the French region of Dauphiné. After a decade of service in that office, and with more than one hundred trials for witchcraft under his belt, he composed a short treatise now known by its opening phrase, "So that the errors of magicians and witches

---

1. Although the exact meaning of this word could vary in different contexts, I generally translate *maleficium* as "witchcraft" and *maleficus* or *malefica* as "witch" throughout this volume, explaining different connotations in notes as needed.

2. See Michael D. Bailey, "Diabolic Magic," in *The Cambridge History of Magic and Witchcraft in the West: From Antiquity to the Present*, ed. David J. Collins (Cambridge: Cambridge University Press, 2015), 361–92.

might be made evident to ignorant people."[3] Beyond describing the forms of witchcraft that he had encountered, his chief concern was to justify secular as opposed to ecclesiastical jurisdiction over this crime. The *Errors of the Gazarii*, on the other hand, was almost certainly written by a church inquisitor. It is a short document focusing on lurid descriptions of the diabolical horrors of witchcraft and witches' assemblies. Its geography is uncertain, but it appears to have been connected to trials in the Aosta valley in northwestern Italy. The next source was also written by a cleric, but it is no brief report. Instead, the Dominican theologian Johannes Nider's *Anthill* is a long moralizing treatise covering an array of topics. Its fifth book, however, specifically addresses "witches and their deceptions." Although Nider wrote *Anthill* mainly in Vienna, most of his information about witchcraft came from western Switzerland, where he had previously served as prior of the Dominican convent in Basel. The final source presented here, *The Vauderie of Lyon*, was again written by a clergyman, most likely a Dominican inquisitor who may have had some direct contact with Nider. It describes the monstrous actions of a sect of witches around the city of Lyon in the southeastern portion of the kingdom of France.

Although each of these sources offers a slightly different perspective on the emerging notion of intensely diabolical, conspiratorial witchcraft, they nevertheless present remarkably similar depictions of certain key elements within that developing stereotype. Above all they agree that witches generally operated in groups, and that they regularly gathered together in the presence of a demonic master to foreswear their faith, engage in devil worship, and commit abominable acts of fornication and cannibalism. Also at their gatherings they brewed potions and poisons needed to work their wicked arts, some of which were distilled from the boiled fat of babies they had murdered, and they received instruction from demons in how to use these noxious

---

3. Pierrette Paravy, "À propos de la genèse médiévale des chasses aux sorcières: Le traite de Claude Tholosan, juge Dauphinois (vers 1436)," *Mélanges de l'École Française de Rome: Moyen Age / Temps Modernes* 91 (1979): 332–79, at 333; Martine Ostorero, Agostino Paravicini Bagliani, and Kathrin Utz Tremp, with Catherine Chène, *L'imaginaire du sabbat: Edition critique des textes les plus anciens (1430 c.–1440 c.)* (Lausanne: Université de Lausanne, 1999), 358, 417.

concoctions. The most common term for such assemblies offered in these texts is "synagogue," but they would eventually come to be known as witches' sabbaths.

The idea of the sabbath was itself a noxious concoction derived from many roots. As the earlier terminology of synagogue suggests, it drew in part on anti-Jewish stereotypes common in medieval Europe. In particular, Christian fears that Jews ritually murdered Christian babies may have fed into the elements of infanticide and cannibalism that frequently figured in accounts of sabbaths.[4] More basically, though, descriptions of these assemblies reflected stereotypes about imagined heretical gatherings that had circulated among ecclesiastical authorities since at least the eleventh century.[5] To this mix were also added a range of beliefs widespread in European folklore about spirits, specters, and other supernatural beings that engaged in nocturnal journeys and raucous nighttime assemblies.[6] These components came together in what, to modern sensibilities, can all too easily appear to be a nonsensical jumble. Yet there was at least some method in the seeming madness of early accounts of the witches' sabbath, and a reason that they all focused on broadly similar points. This can best be understood by tracing certain historical developments that provide

---

4. See R. Po-Chia Hsia, *The Myth of Ritual Murder: Jews and Magic in Reformation Germany* (New Haven: Yale University Press, 1988), esp. 1–13 for background. On the origin of the stereotype, see E. M. Rose, *The Murder of William of Norwich: The Origins of the Blood Libel in Medieval Europe* (Oxford: Oxford University Press, 2015). On witches murdering children, see Richard Kieckhefer, "Avenging the Blood of Children: Anxiety over Child Victims and the Origins of the European Witch Trials," in *The Devil, Heresy and Witchcraft in the Middle Ages: Essays in Honor of Jeffrey B. Russell*, ed. Alberto Ferreiro (Leiden: Brill, 1998), 91–109, esp. 100–7 for sources translated here.

5. For one such diabolized assembly that supposedly took place in 1022, see Walter L. Wakefield and Austin P. Evans, *Heresies of the High Middle Ages* (New York: Columbia University Press, 1969), 78–79. On the connection of witchcraft to heresy, see Jeffrey B. Russell, *Witchcraft in the Middle Ages* (Ithaca: Cornell University Press, 1972); Kathrin Utz Tremp, *Von der Häresie zur Hexerei: "Wirkliche" und imaginäre Sekten im Spätmittelalter* (Hannover: Hahnsche Buchhandlung, 2008).

6. Famously, but problematically, see Carlo Ginzburg, *Ecstasies: Deciphering the Witches' Sabbath*, trans. Raymond Rosenthal (New York: Penguin, 1991).

the necessary context in which to understand the idea of the sabbath as articulated across all these sources.

LEGAL AND THEOLOGICAL CONTEXT

Readers might be surprised, in a collection of texts relating to witchcraft, to find relatively little discussion of spells, charms, and actual acts of bewitchment. Most of the harmful magic supposedly performed by witches is described only briefly, at best, in these sources. People are injured or made ill through spells or poisons, both men and women (and sometimes animals) are rendered infertile and incapable of sexual reproduction, crops are damaged or stolen out of fields, lightning and hail are called down from the heavens. Such magical crimes are not what stirred these authors, however, at least not directly. What most agitated them was the idea that witches were now acting not as individual malefactors but as members of diabolically orchestrated cults. The *Errors of the Gazarii*, for example, was less concerned about weather magic per se than about how groups of witches supposedly flew to the top of certain mountain peaks to gather the ice that would rain down on their neighbors' fields as hail. Likewise, *The Vauderie of Lyon* cared less that witches could "cause sickness in both people and animals" than that they did so through "powders made through the demon's craft," which they concocted at their gatherings.

Although advanced by lay as well as clerical writers, and acted on by secular as well as ecclesiastical courts, the notion that witches functioned as agents of a diabolical conspiracy was rooted in theological concepts about the nature of demonic magic that had been developing since the thirteenth century, and in inquisitorial legal structures that had developed to root out heresies at roughly the same time. As noted already, Christian authorities had always linked most forms of magic to demonic power. Only in the twelfth and especially the thirteenth centuries, however, did scholastic theologians develop systematic arguments about the actual scope of demonic abilities. Thinkers such as William of Auvergne (d. 1249) and Thomas Aquinas (d. 1274) worked out in precise terms how demons, as spiritual beings, could directly affect the physical world. This ran counter to an older notion that demons acted primarily through trickery and deceit, which endured into the era of the witches' sabbath mainly in debates (introduced in more detail in the next section) about whether witches really flew to their nocturnal assemblies or whether that was merely a demonic illusion. Whereas some authorities held to older ideas, by the early fifteenth century many theologians used testimony given by accused witches themselves, usually under torture or other coercion, to prove the physical reality of demonic actions.[7]

As authorities worked out how witches and other practitioners of harmful magic relied on demons to achieve real results, they also had to establish what working relationship existed between witches and demons. If a human witch was merely a vessel through which a demon wrought harm in the world, perhaps she was not really to blame for her crimes. If, however, she willingly placed herself in a demon's service in order to gain her terrible powers, offering it her devotion and worship, then she could be judged a heretic as well as a witch. This conflation occurred mainly in the fourteenth century. In 1320, Pope John XXII assembled a special papal commission to determine whether demonic magic was inherently heretical. The point was actually quite complicated since heresy was, most basically, an act of volition—a thought crime that involved holding some kind of belief fundamentally opposed to Christian doctrine. Magic, on the other hand, was an action intended to achieve supposedly tangible results. Nevertheless, John's commission determined that anyone who engaged with demons in order to perform a magical act necessarily elevated those demons to a place of honor and worship, which no faithful Christian should ever do.[8] In 1326, John issued a proclamation excommunicating all practitioners of demonic magic from the church.[9]

7. Walter Stephens, *Demon Lovers: Witchcraft, Sex, and the Crisis of Belief* (Chicago: University of Chicago Press, 2002).

8. Alain Boureau, *Satan the Heretic: The Birth of Demonology in the Medieval West*, trans. Teresa Lavender Fagan (Chicago: University of Chicago Press, 2006), esp. 8–67.

9. Joseph Hansen, *Quellen und Untersuchungen zur Geschichte des Hexenwahns und der Hexenverfolgung im Mittelalter* (1901; repr., Hildesheim: Georg Olms, 1963), 5–6; for an English translation, see Alan Charles Kors and Edward Peters, *Witchcraft in Europe, 400–1700: A Documentary History*, 2nd ed. (Philadelphia: University of Pennsylvania Press, 2001), 119–20.

Yet the issue was not so easily settled. Although John XXII himself instructed inquisitors in southern France to begin investigating cases involving demonic magic in 1320, a decade later he ordered them to stop and send all the case materials they had gathered to the papal court for review.[10] Moreover, John's 1326 pronouncement does not appear to have entered into church law at this time. It only achieved real significance fifty years later, in 1376, when the Dominican inquisitor Nicolau Eimeric included it in his great manual *Directorium inquisitorum*.[11] The inquisitorial courts that became involved in cases of witchcraft in the early 1400s were, therefore, still in the process of establishing their jurisdiction over this crime. This was why it was so imperative for them to stress the intensely diabolical nature of the new stereotype of witchcraft entailed in the sabbath, as well as its collective nature. A heretic could operate in isolation, of course, but it was much easier to prove heresy if it supposedly manifested in collective actions, such as participation in demonic cults that required overt apostasy from the Christian faith.

The idea of witches assembling in large groups also fed into the fears of secular authorities. They could now imagine witches as constituting an organized social and perhaps even political threat as agents of the devil working to undermine the stable order of Christian society.[12] This is how witches appeared in the Swiss chronicler Hans Fründ's account about their activities in the region of Valais, where he feared that, if left unchecked, they "could have raised up a king from among them." Likewise the royal magistrate Claude Tholosan, in his explicit argument for secular jurisdiction over witchcraft, presented witches as having committed treason against the French crown.

10. Hansen, *Quellen*, 4–5, 6–7.

11. For the development of inquisitorial thought on magic and witchcraft, see Michael D. Bailey, "From Sorcery to Witchcraft: Clerical Conceptions of Magic in the Later Middle Ages," *Speculum* 76 (2001): 960–90; Derek Hill, *Inquisition in the Fourteenth Century: The Manuals of Bernard Gui and Nicholas Eymerich* (York: York Medieval Press, 2019), 176–93.

12. On witchcraft as social and political as well as theological deviance, see Richard Kieckhefer, "Witchcraft, Necromancy, and Sorcery as Heresy," in *Chasses aux sorcières et démonologie: Entre discours et pratiques (XIVe–XVIIe siècles)*, ed. Martine Ostorero, Georg Modestin, and Kathrin Utz Tremp (Florence: SISMEL, 2010), 133–53.

Church authorities in the early fifteenth century did not need to look far for a major and terrifying example of a politically disruptive heresy. After the execution of the Czech clerical reformer Jan Hus at a church council in 1415, his followers, known as Hussites, rose up in the kingdom of Bohemia. The church branded them heretics, but they were as much a political revolution as a religious movement, and for the next several decades they both defended themselves against crusading armies and launched retributive military forays deep into the surrounding German empire.[13] Of the authors here, Johannes Nider most directly engaged with the Hussite heresy, in addition to writing about witchcraft (although it should be noted that he drew no explicit connection between them).[14]

This legal and theological context helps explain the extensive and often outlandish accusations made in these sources about witches' gross moral degeneracy and especially the amount of space spent alleging their desecration of sacraments and sacramental items, such as the Eucharist and the cross. The attention lavished on the presence of demons at the sabbath and on witches' physical encounters with them, above all their carnal encounters, should also be understood in this light. So too should the passages devoted to witches' supposedly explicit declarations of subservience to their demonic masters. Whether they were laymen or clerics, the authors of all these sources strove to emphasize such points, rather than just the acts of harmful magic that witches supposedly performed against their neighbors. They intended their descriptions of witches' sabbaths to paint a picture of extreme moral and social deviance in order to bolster a particular way of understanding demonic power in the world and to justify the actions that they or the institutions they served sought to take against the alleged agents of that power.

---

13. Howard Kaminsky, *A History of the Hussite Revolution* (Berkeley: University of California Press, 1967); František M. Bartoš, *The Hussite Revolution, 1424–1437*, ed. and trans. John M. Klassen (New York: Columbia University Press, 1986).

14. Michael D. Bailey, *Battling Demons: Witchcraft, Heresy, and Reform in the Late Middle Ages* (University Park: Pennsylvania State University Press, 2003), 57–64.

This is not to say that these sources absolutely agreed on all aspects of witchcraft and the sabbath. Indeed, it is often where they disagree to some extent that they become most interesting to modern readers, for here we can see stereotypes still in the process of coalescing and ideas that were by no means fully accepted at this time being either contested or defended. In order to highlight some of their similarities as well as notable differences, let me now outline what I see as the main components of the witches' sabbath as depicted in these sources and draw some key comparisons.

ELEMENTS OF THE SABBATH

Demonic Assemblies

As I have already stressed, the most essential component of the sabbath was the idea that witches were organized into a sect that met regularly in the presence of a demon or devil[15] in order to worship that creature and perform nefarious acts under its direction. All five of these sources agreed on this point. Nider's *Anthill* was the most prosaic, stating only that witches often gathered in local churches "on a Sunday before the holy water is consecrated" in order to initiate new members into the sect. Fründ's report indicated that they "gathered together at schools in secret places," but he also reported how witches confessed that "the evil spirit carried them at night from one mountain to another," and this could easily be taken to suggest that the schools themselves met on mountain tops. Claude Tholosan described how witches believed that they would "journey physically during the night, especially on Thursdays and Saturdays, with a troop of devils," and that they would assemble in "one particular place" to hold a "synagogue." He also noted that "they declare that they travel far, some on a staff anointed with children's fat . . . and some on beasts and brooms." The

---

15. Medieval sources switch back and forth between *demon* and *diabolus* quite freely, with *diabolus* frequently meaning merely a devil rather than the devil. Latin almost never employs articles, so this distinction is sometimes uncertain. In discussing sources, I typically use whichever word was used in the source itself, despite this possible confusion.

Errors of the Gazarii was quite specific about how the devil provided witches with "a small box full of unguent and a staff and everything else [needed] to go to the synagogue." *The Vauderie of Lyon* offered the most detail, describing how witches traveled at night, "some walking, some riding on a malign spirit that appears to them in some horrible form, others on a staff." Their assemblies were "sometimes quite far away and distant" but most often took place at secluded crossroads. They were usually held on Thursday nights, beginning around sunset and lasting until the first church bells would ring at dawn.

Night Flight and Nighttime Revels

Ironically, given that all these sources agreed on the fact that witches gathered at diabolical assemblies, the point on which they most dramatically disagreed was how witches might travel to these conventicles, and whether they were actually real or merely diabolical delusions. Here the most multifaceted position came from Johannes Nider. He generally presented witches' gatherings as local affairs that would not require any extraordinary means of locomotion. Although he never expressly denied the possibility of witches flying to a sabbath, in the second book of his *Anthill*, dealing with "revelations" rather than "witches and their deceptions," he did present a story about a Dominican friar who disabused a foolish old woman of her belief that she sometimes flew through the night with the pagan goddess Diana. This was a direct echo of the famous canon *Episcopi* (so called for its first word, "Bishops"), a document of church law dating from the tenth century that declared such flight to be illusory.[16] In the fifteenth century, *Episcopi* became a fundamental basis for skepticism on the part of church authorities about all claims that witches flew or were otherwise transported by demons to sabbaths.[17] Seeming to draw on that line of thinking, Nider also briefly mentioned how two specific witches would "travel from place to place, *so they think*, through the

16. Hansen, *Quellen*, 38–39; translated in (among other places) Kors and Peters, *Witchcraft in Europe*, 60–63.

17. Martine Ostorero, *Le diable au sabbat: Littérature démonologique et sorcellerie (1440–1460)* (Florence: SISMEL, 2011), 567–720.

air" (my emphasis). These particular witches, however, were not traveling to sabbaths. Moreover, Nider included in the first chapter of the fifth book of the *Anthill* an account of apparently real, physical transportation of a human by spirit beings, namely, of a knight from the Rhineland who rode in the course of one night to Jerusalem and back with an army of the dead. So whatever skepticism Nider held about witches' flight, he did not seem to think that such modes of transportation were inherently impossible.

Hans Fründ, as noted already, described witches confessing "how the evil spirit carried them at night from one mountain to another, and how he taught them to make ointments with which they would anoint chairs and then ride on them from one village to another and from one castle to another." His account might seem, therefore, to accept flight as a reality, but it should be noted that all this was simply Fründ reporting what potentially deluded witches had themselves confessed. He also immediately followed this description of flight with an account of witches supposedly transforming into wolves. This section of his text can be read as indicating a bit more skepticism, for it stated that the witches only "thought" that they had transformed and "did not know any differently," and that they now "seemed to be wolves" both to themselves and other people. Metamorphosis and flight were often linked together in the minds of skeptics, not necessarily as impossible activities, but as far more likely a matter of diabolical deception than of real transformation or transportation.

Claude Tholosan left no doubt about his skepticism. He stated explicitly that the devil merely "deludes [witches] in dreams such that they believe [themselves] to journey physically during the night . . . with a troop of devils," or to fly on animals, brooms, or staffs. The *Errors of the Gazarii* took the opposite stance, leaving seemingly little doubt that witches had been "proven" to fly on brooms or staffs. Not only did they fly to their assemblies, but they also carried ice that they had harvested from mountaintops "through the air on stormy days, by means of a staff," in order to cause hailstorms. Since the destruction wrought by these storms was quite real, there could be no doubt about the reality of witches' flight. It should be noted, however, that the entire section about carrying ice was a later addition to the *Errors of the Gazarii*, and the subtitle stating that witches had been "proven" to fly on brooms or staffs may have been added by someone other than the original author as well.[18]

The Vauderie of Lyon presented an interesting twist on these conflicting positions. It seemed to accept as a reality that witches "go out at night, following after Satan—some walking, some riding on a malign spirit that appears to them in some horrible form, others on a staff," and that they were "borne through the air and also over great distances." One copy of the text then went further, explaining how the devil employed "certain literate men" who had been seduced into the sect of witches in order to "secretly exhort or even to some degree publicly proclaim that these disgraceful things do not really take place either in effect or in fact." Instead, they themselves argued, falsely, for the skeptical position that the sabbath took place "only in dreams and fantastical visions, and that it is nothing more than an imaginary delusion." They did this so that people would then be inclined to take all the other terrible crimes committed by witches less seriously as well.

Closely related to the issue of flight to a sabbath was the matter of witches' supposed nocturnal celebrations held in the cellars of wealthy people's houses. Both involved witches being transported by demons. Moreover, notions of spirit beings often called the "good ones" or the "good ladies" traveling through the night and entering houses existed in European folklore long before the notion of the witches' sabbath began to coalesce. These spirits could often be placated by offerings of food, or they might ransack the houses if no offerings were made. Such beliefs mingled with those about other kinds of night-traveling spirit troops and appear to have contributed to ideas of the sabbath in many ways.[19]

Of the sources presented here, only Nider failed to mention witches intruding into cellars and plundering stocks of food and drink, although he did relate a story drawn from the life of the early Christian

18. Even though it appears in the earliest known manuscript copy of the text, that copy is assumed not to be the original.

19. See Claude Lecouteaux, *Phantom Armies of the Night: The Wild Hunt and the Ghostly Processions of the Undead*, trans. Jon E. Graham (Rochester, VT: Inner Traditions, 1999), esp. 8–23; Ronald Hutton, *The Witch: A History of Fear, from Ancient Times to the Present* (New Haven: Yale University Press, 2017), esp. 120–46.

saint Germanus of Auxerre, who had died a millennium earlier in the mid-fifth century. Once, while traveling through what was then Gaul, the saint found himself staying in a house where the table had been set at night with food and drink for the "good women." He realized, however, that these women were just demons in disguise, and he commanded them to reveal their true nature to the people who had foolishly been leaving these offerings.

Regarding fifteenth-century witches, Claude Tholosan was the most explicitly skeptical about the reality of their nighttime intrusions, stating that witches only "think that they eat and drink in houses that the devils open." The *Errors of the Gazarii* appears to have been the most credulous, stating as a matter of fact that "the devil leads them to the homes of powerful prelates, nobles, burghers, and others, in which he knows there is food and wine matching their wishes and desires, opening the cellars of the aforesaid powerful people to them around the third hour of the night and leading them in." Fründ's report also seems to have accepted the reality of these nighttime revels, stating that witches would "gather in the cellars of the people who had the best wine." When asked about physical evidence for these revels—that is, whether stores of wine would be visibly reduced in a cellar into which they had supposedly intruded—the witches "answered and said yes, there was less [wine] in the casks from which they had drunk." *The Vauderie of Lyon* then presented what might have served as a possible response to skeptical challenges along these lines, namely, that witches might sometimes confess to breaking into cellars in which stores of wine did not later appear to have been reduced in any measure. This, however, would be because, after they had had their fill of the wine, "first the demon and then all these wretched idolaters climb up on the same barrel from which they drank and one by one they urinate in it and try to fill the vessel up again with their filth."

Entering the Devil's Service

Wherever witches gathered, a demon would manifest at their assemblies, although it might do so in a variety of forms. Once again, Nider's *Anthill* offered the most reticent description, saying only that a demon would appear "visibly in the assumed likeness of a human being." Tholosan stated that the devil "usually appears to them in the form of a human being," but somehow translucent. That is, "his body, like glass, does not block the rays of the sun" and "he casts no shadow when facing the sun." He could also take on the form of "many different animals," and other sources stressed these animal forms. Fründ stated that "the evil spirit appeared to them most often in the form of a black animal, sometimes in the form of a bear, sometimes in the form of a ram or in a terrible evil form." According to the *Errors of the Gazarii*, the "enemy appears sometimes in the form of a black cat, sometimes in the form of a human being, although imperfect somehow, or in the guise of another animal, but most commonly in the guise of a black cat."

By far the most horrific descriptions of a presiding demon come from *The Vauderie of Lyon*. Here the creature would often appear to the assembled witches "in the form of a very repulsive man, that is, black, completely covered with hair and bristles, with horns, having a monstrous, drawn out, and twisted shape." The text went on to describe that shape over the course of several wonderfully twisted lines. It concluded in agreement with other sources, however, noting that the devil also "is accustomed to appear in the form and likeness of some beast, but always unclean, foul, and extremely vile, such as a goat, fox, large dog, ram, wolf, cat, badger, bull, or something else of this sort."

In whatever form he took, the presiding demon received homage, oaths, and sometimes offerings representing the witches' subservience to him. According to Hans Fründ, not only did witches have to deny God and the church before the "evil spirit," but "they had to pay him an annual tribute in various ways, namely, with a black sheep or lamb, [or] with a measure of oats." Sometimes they had to offer some part of their own bodies to be collected by the demon after they had died. Claude Tholosan described an elaborate ceremony in which initiates into the witches' sect had to deny God and the church and then drink from a vessel in which the devil had urinated. They also had to bare their naked posteriors to heaven "as an insult to God" and spit and trample on a cross that they had drawn in the dirt. They would then have to "kneel and kiss the devil" on his mouth, and they also promised him their "body and soul, along with one of their children, most often their firstborn." Thereafter, they were compelled to "make an annual tribute to him, in the aforesaid way, on the day when they [first] subjugated themselves."

Other sources echoed many of these elements. The *Errors of the Gazarii*, for example, noted that after swearing fealty to the devil, and "as a sign of homage," a new witch would kiss the devil, not on the mouth but on the "ass or anus." The initiate would also pledge to the devil "as a sign of tribute one of the limbs of his body after death." Beyond even this, the new witch would enter into an explicit contract with the devil written in blood. According to this source, "the devil draws blood from the seduced person's left hand with a certain instrument, and with this blood writes certain things on a parchment, which he then keeps with him, and many from the sect have seen this, as they have testified." Compared to such elaborate rites, the accounts of demon worship in Nider's *Anthill* appear relatively tame. He noted only that a new witch had to "swear to this demon to deny Christianity, never to adore the Eucharist, and to trample on the cross whenever he could do so secretly." Slightly later, Nider repeated that a new witch had to "deny Christ, his faith, baptism, and the universal church," and then had to "give homage" to the demon.

Once again *The Vauderie of Lyon* provided the most extensive descriptions of how witches entered the devil's service. "They do this," it stated, "with suppliant prostration and kneeling or genuflection, with clasped and clapping hands, and by kissing that one [the demon] on some part of his body, usually his backside or posterior." One copy of the text added graphically, "they affirm that during this kiss they smell a very foul odor." Of course, witches would also "deny the Christian faith and everything pertaining to it, especially holy baptism and all the sacraments of the church," and they explicitly rejected "Christ our redeemer, and the most blessed Virgin Mary, and all the saints of God." Like Claude Tholosan and Johannes Nider, the author of *The Vauderie* described witches trampling on the cross, but in this text they also stole the Eucharist wafer from church so that they could abuse it "by trampling it irreverently with their feet, by vilely defiling it with their spit . . . [and] by pouring urine and their other unspeakable excrements on it." Rather more prosaically, they also had to "deliver without fail to the devil their master some tribute of wheat, barley, oats, rye, millet, eggs, and other things of this sort, generally once a month or at certain times during the year."

The most practically important oath that witches would swear upon entering the devil's service was that they would never reveal anything about the sect of witches to any authorities. Fründ noted that "they would not go to confess to any priest what they had accomplished through their art." The *Errors of the Gazarii* stated that a new witch had to swear "that even unto death he will not reveal the secrets of the aforesaid sect." Claude Tholosan expanded on this, detailing that they could not "reveal anything about themselves to ministers of the church or to priests, or even to the ministers of justice." In exchange, the devil "sometimes protects and strengthens them during interrogations, so that they do not feel the torture." Likewise *The Vauderie of Lyon* explained that "the aforesaid heretics declare and promise to their demon and to each other that they will in no way accuse each other or in any way disclose their witchcraft in court or elsewhere." The devil then "hardens them" so that they "remain impervious" to even the most "diligent" interrogation. Johannes Nider did not explain this mechanism outright, but he did relate one case of a captured witch who initially resisted questioning but then confessed freely. The witch himself explained "that on the other two days he was restrained by the devices of demons from being able to confess under torture." A Mass dedicated to Mary had been celebrated on the third day of his interrogation, however, which had liberated him from the demon's thrall.

Infanticide and Cannibalism

Perhaps the most viscerally horrific behavior described in these sources involved witches supposedly killing and eating babies at or in connection to their sabbaths. Medieval sensibilities recoiled from such grotesque acts as much as modern ones now do. Johannes Nider reported many crimes committed by witches in the Alpine territory of the city of Bern, but it was the fact that "thirteen babies had been devoured by witches within a short period of time" there that, according to him, "so harshly inflamed" public sentiment against them. Such murderous rites could occur in several ways. First, children, often the witches' own offspring, could be sacrificed as a tribute to the devil. The bodies of murdered babies could be boiled down into fat or grease and used in poisons or to slather on the brooms or staffs that, in some accounts, carried witches to the sabbath. Witches might also kill children, of course, simply as an evil act in its own right. Often these elements blended together in the accounts.

Hans Fründ, for example, described how witches "killed their own children and roasted and ate them, [or] boiled them and took them to their assembly and ate them," but also how they would smear poisonous material on their hands and then secretly touch children, causing them to waste away. According to Claude Tholosan, witches would sacrifice their own children to the devil, especially their firstborn, but they would also use the boiled fat from both their own children and others whom they had killed and devoured at their gatherings to perform further witchcraft. The *Errors of the Gazarii* stated that all new witches had to pledge to the devil that they would kill as many children as they could and bring the corpses to their assemblies. There, they would roast or boil these bodies and eat them, after drawing out the fat with which they anointed the staffs on which they flew. Slightly later, the text described how witches typically committed such murders, creeping into houses at night and strangling or suffocating babies in their cradles. They would not take the bodies at that point but would wait until after they were buried, then dig them up and carry them to the sabbath.

Johannes Nider, in his *Anthill*, described an identical process. First, witches would "lie in wait for babies who have not yet been baptized . . . [or] protected with the sign of the cross and prayers." After killing them at night in their cribs or even lying in bed with their parents, so that the babies would appear "to have been smothered or killed in another way," the witches stole them from out of their graves, took them to their gatherings, and "boil them in a cauldron until . . . nearly all the flesh is rendered such that it can be slurped up or drunk." But Nider also presented a more restrained account of a witch killing children, devoid of the lurid horrors of cannibalism or the sabbath. Describing the activity of one witch, who at no point was associated explicitly with any conspiratorial sect, he stated that "he killed around seven of [a certain] woman's babies in the womb through his witchcraft, one after the other, so that for many years she always miscarried." This witch likewise afflicted all the farm animals belonging to this woman and her husband. Here we see concern not about infanticide per se, but about witches affecting fertility and reproduction in general.

The Vauderie of Lyon touched on all these points. It recounted how witches would kill children as a sacrifice to the devil and then make an unguent from their bodies to smear on their staffs for flight. It also described how witches afflicted fertility, causing pregnant women to miscarry, or even smothering children at the moment of birth, as they were "delivering [them] from their mother's womb in the manner of midwives." The idea that midwives were often suspected of being witches has gained a great deal of traction in popular conceptions about late medieval and early modern witchcraft. This is mainly because the idea of midwife witches was championed so vigorously in the infamous *Malleus maleficarum* (*Hammer of Witches*), written by yet another Dominican inquisitor in 1486.[20] In fact, however, careful study has shown that midwives were typically respected members of their communities and were not accused of witchcraft at especially high rates compared to other women.[21]

Sex with the Devil and the Gender of Witches

The notion of witchcraft as a highly sexualized crime, and a starkly gendered one, was also evident in this period, although as with midwife witches, these notions reached their apogee half a century later with the *Malleus maleficarum* and its famous declaration that "everything" about witchcraft stemmed from "carnal lust, which in them [women] is insatiable."[22] This idea was present in some of these earlier sources, but it was not so strongly developed. Hans Fründ, for example, did not include lust at all among the motivating factors that he felt drove

20. Heinrich Kramer, *Malleus maleficarum* 1.11, 2.1.13.

21. David Harley, "Historians as Demonologists: The Myth of the Midwife-Witch," *Social History of Medicine* 3 (1990): 1–26; Mary E. Wiesner, *Women and Gender in Early Modern Europe* (Cambridge: Cambridge University Press, 1993), 127–28.

22. Kramer, *Malleus* 1.6.

people to become witches. Instead he stressed greed and a desire for power to inflict harm on their enemies. Perhaps not surprisingly, then, his accounts of witches' assemblies contained no mention of orgiastic revels or sex with demons. Nider's *Anthill* also did not describe any sexual activity occurring at witches' assemblies, although he noted that witches could drive other men and women to excessive carnal desires,[23] and he related many stories of women afflicted by demons in the form of incubi.[24] He clearly thought that witchcraft was interwoven with carnal lust, but he nowhere explicitly stated that lust caused people to become witches.

Claude Tholosan briefly mentioned that the people most likely to be drawn into witchcraft were those "inclined to vengeance or sensual pleasure," and he explicitly included sex as an element of the sabbath. At the devil's command, the assembled witches "have carnal knowledge of each other, and they mingle with demons, sometimes even against nature." *The Vauderie of Lyon* also described orgiastic sex as a feature of the sabbath, stating that "during this dance, at a signal known to them, every man and woman lies down and mingles together in the manner of brutes or sodomites. And even the devil, as an incubus or succubus, takes whatever man or woman he wishes." Yet, although *The Vauderie* discussed the factors that drove people to become witches at some length, it did not explicitly include lust among them. Instead, it agreed with Fründ that people were driven into witchcraft by "desire for . . . riches, luxuries, and honors," as well as "vengeance against their enemies."

Among these early sources, the *Errors of the Gazarii* was most direct in its statement that people became witches partly in order to "take pleasure wantonly in the sexual act," as well as owing to greed and a desire for power. The *Errors* also described orgies at witches' assemblies similar to those described in *The Vauderie of Lyon*. At a particular point during the gathering, the "presiding devil" would give a signal, and then the witches would "join together carnally, man with woman, or man with man, and sometimes father with daughter, son with mother, brother with sister, and with the proper order of nature scarcely being observed." Still, it is notable that, in terms of "revels" and

23. *Anthill* 5.5.   24. Mainly in *Anthill* 5.9–10.

"pleasures" taking place as part of an assembly of witches, only three texts (Tholosan's treatise, *Errors of the Gazarii*, and *The Vauderie of Lyon*) mentioned sexual orgies, whereas four (those three plus Fründ's report) described feasting and drinking in cellars.

In terms of any explicit gendering of witchcraft, most of these early sources were quite reticent. This is somewhat surprising because general evidence from across Europe for the first several decades of the fifteenth century shows that women were being accused of witchcraft at about twice the rate as men were.[25] That percentage is confirmed for our region by statistics drawn from trials in Dauphiné.[26] Yet among the sources presented here, both Fründ's report and the *Errors of the Gazarii* stressed in their opening lines that witches could be "both women and men" and were "of either sex." *The Vauderie of Lyon* likewise stated that witches were "both men and women" just a few lines into its text. It did at one point refer specifically to "some women from this sect" who had confessed to having sex with demons, and at another point it mentioned "that there are women among them" (that is, in the sect of witches) who were adept at magically stealing milk from either human wet nurses or their neighbors' cows. Yet it should be noted that both these references are found only in one slightly later copy of the text. In *So That the Errors of Magicians and Witches Might Be Made Evident to Ignorant People*, Claude Tholosan made no comment on the gender of witches at all.

Johannes Nider's *Anthill*, on the other hand, argued at length that women were more susceptible than men to the lure of witchcraft, or at least to the temptations of demons. It was, in fact, the first authoritative source to present this argument in such a direct form, and it would profoundly influence the similar argument made fifty years later in the *Malleus maleficarum*.[27] Yet Nider's discussion of gender deserves careful attention. I have included it here among the sections

---

25. Richard Kieckhefer, *European Witch Trials: Their Foundations in Popular and Learned Culture, 1300–1500* (Berkeley: University of California Press, 1976), 118–25.

26. Pierrette Paravy, *De la chrétienté romaine a la Réforme en Dauphiné:*

Évêques, fidèles et deviants (vers 1340–vers 1530), 2 vols. (Rome: École Française de Rome, 1993), 2:782–83, 823.

27. Compare *Anthill* 5.8 to *Malleus* 1.6.

of the *Anthill* to be translated because of its eventual influence on gendered conceptions of witchcraft. When Nider came to discuss gender, however, it was not at all clear that he was still describing the sort of witch who belonged to a conspiratorial sect and attended a sabbath.

In most of his discussions of witchcraft, Nider referred to "witches of both sexes." He typically used male nouns and pronouns to refer to them generically (as was normal in Latin), and his specific stories focused as often on male witches as on female ones. When in *Anthill* 5.8 the "lazy student" who was his interlocutor asked whether there were "in our time some good men who are deceived by female magicians or witches," Nider responded with three examples of women who dressed as men and sought to influence the politics of their day. The most famous of these was Joan of Arc, who revived French resistance against the invading English and turned the tide of the Hundred Years War. Nider judged her to have been in the service of demons, but he carefully called her only a female magician (*maga*) rather than a witch (*malefica*). Some of the other women he discussed in relation to this question were labeled "magicians or witches" (*magae vel maelficae*). It is in response to these specific cases, and not to the horrors of the witches' sabbath, that the lazy student declared, "I cannot wonder enough how the fragile sex dares to rush into such audacities," and Nider then launched into his explanation of why women were more susceptible than men to demonic temptation and more prone to wickedness.

SPREAD AND INFLUENCE

The depictions of conspiratorial witchcraft and the witches' sabbath that appeared in these five important sources from the 1430s were by no means entirely uniform. Nevertheless, they presented a clear set of stereotypes that were in the process of coalescing. These were not the only stereotypes of witchcraft taking shape at this time. In northern Italy a somewhat different set of beliefs became predominant. In particular, they stressed an image of the witch as a vampiric monster related to deeply rooted Mediterranean folklore about night-stalking creatures like the *strix* and *lamia*, whose origins stretched back to classical mythology.[28] Ultimately, however, the northern stereotype would become more widely influential, as it spread during the remainder of the fifteenth century into France, Germany, and the Low Countries.[29] By the early sixteenth century, it would even spread, albeit temporarily, into Italy as well.[30]

Over subsequent centuries and across Europe, stereotypes of witchcraft were never static or stable. Demonologists continued to debate the real or illusory nature of night flight and therefore of the sabbath itself. Trial records frequently show that ordinary people, and many magistrates as well, did not care about the supposed diabolical aspects of witchcraft nearly so much as the practical harm that they believed could be done through malefic magic. Yet it is equally evident that the imagined horrors of the sabbath contributed in many contexts to the powerful fear of witchcraft that gripped Europe for several centuries, and especially to the most vicious aspects of witch-hunting. Indeed, the basic mechanism by which a hunt could expand and possibly spiral out of control—the insistence that accused witches name others who could then be hauled into court—is inconceivable without the underlying notion that witches were members of large sects, their malevolent actions orchestrated by demons or by the devil himself. This is the idea that we can see emerging so clearly in these sources, on its way to reshape one grim part of Europe's mental landscape for the next several hundred years.

SELECTION AND SEQUENCE OF THE TEXTS

Scholars have long known about the increasingly diabolized, conspiratorial conception of witchcraft that began to emerge in the early fifteenth century.[31] In particular, a team of scholars based at

28. On these two stereotypes, see Richard Kieckhefer, "Mythologies of Witchcraft in the Fifteenth Century," *Magic, Ritual, and Witchcraft* 1 (2006): 79–108.

29. For the "second generation" of northern demonologists active in this diffusion, see Ostorero, *Diable au sabbat.*

30. Tamar Herzig, "Bridging North and South: Inquisitorial Networks and Witchcraft Theory on the Eve of the Reformation," *Journal of Early Modern Studies* 12 (2008): 361–82.

31. A pathbreaking study in this regard was Kieckhefer, *European Witch Trials.* My own work in this area began with Michael D. Bailey, "The Medieval

the University of Lausanne spent more than two decades carefully researching the early trials and texts that chronicled this development in western Switzerland, northwestern Italy, and southeastern France.[32] Those familiar with their work will immediately recognize the debt that this volume owes to their pioneering publication, *L'imaginaire du sabbat*, in which they edited five major early sources that described witches' sabbaths.

Imaginaire also provided French translations of all those sources, four of which are reproduced here. My contribution has been to render them into English, in which they have not previously been available except in scattered form and often only in brief excerpts. I have also made one major alteration to the selection of texts in *Imaginaire*. I have dropped its excerpt from book 4 of the French courtier Martin Le Franc's long poem *The Defender of Ladies* (*Le Champion des Dames*) in favor of the anonymous treatise *The Vauderie of Lyon*. Recent research has allowed this text, long thought to have been composed around 1460, to be redated to the very end of the 1430s, and so to take its place among the earliest accounts of the witches' sabbath.[33] Written by a Dominican inquisitor in Lyon, it fits more directly with the other sources presented here, all of which were composed by clerical or lay officials who had some connection to witch-hunting in this region. *The Defender*, by contrast, emerged from the so-called *querelle des femmes*, the literary "debate over women," in the fifteenth century. Only one section of the long poem addressed witchcraft. It offers an important and in some ways unique perspective on developing stereotypes, but it also requires a different kind of analysis and invites different comparisons than the other sources translated here. Ultimately I decided that its exclusion was regrettable but warranted.[34]

Concept of the Witches' Sabbath," *Exemplaria* 8 (1996): 419–39.

32. For an overview, see Kathrin Utz Tremp, "Witches' Brooms and Magic Ointments: Twenty Years of Witchcraft Research at the University of Lausanne (1989–2009)," *Magic, Ritual, and Witchcraft* 5 (2010): 173–87.

33. See note 43 below.

34. For a full edition of the witchcraft material with commentary, see Ostorero et al., *Imaginaire*, 441–508. For an English translation, see Martin Le Franc, *The Trial of Womankind: A Rhyming Translation of Book IV of the Fifteenth-Century* Le Champion des Dames, ed. and trans. Steven Millen Taylor (Jefferson, NC: McFarland, 2005), 90–113.

I have arranged the sources in a manner as straightforwardly chronological as possible, although of course there is almost always some level of uncertainty when dating medieval texts. The earliest of these sabbath accounts is undoubtedly Hans Fründ's report about a series of trials in the region of Valais that began in 1428 and lasted about a year and a half. The report itself was most likely written quite soon after that, perhaps in late 1429 or 1430.[35] The wave of trials actually continued in Valais until 1436.[36] That same year was when Claude Tholosan appears to have written *So That the Errors of Magicians and Witches Might Be Made Evident to Ignorant People*, after a decade of presiding over witch trials in the region of Dauphiné.[37]

With the *Errors of the Gazarii*, exact chronological placement becomes more complicated. The tract was long thought to date to around 1450.[38] Only after a second copy of the text was discovered in a manuscript that otherwise recorded actions of the ecclesiastical Council of Basel down to 1437 could the *Errors* be redated to the 1430s.[39] It also emerged that the first known copy was actually a later, expanded version of the text, which was itself subsequently redated to late 1438 or thereafter.[40] This creates problems situating the *Errors* in relation to Nider's *Anthill*. We know that Nider began writing that long work perhaps as early as 1436, although he did not finish it until 1438, the year in which he died. He probably wrote most of his accounts of witchcraft in 1437/38.[41] One might argue, therefore, that the *Anthill* should precede the *Errors of the Gazarii*, especially since I present here the fuller, later version of the *Errors*, which was written after the *Anthill* was completed. On the other hand, the original version of the *Errors* had been circulating since early 1437, possibly before Nider even began his treatise, and definitely before he finished it.

The Vauderie of Lyon has also been subject to some dramatic redating. For a long time it was known only through a single copy contained in a manuscript that collected other outbreaks of witchcraft

---

35. Ostorero et al., *Imaginaire*, 26.
36. Ibid., 70.
37. Paravy, "À propos de la genèse," 333; Ostorero et al., *Imaginaire*, 358, 417.
38. Hansen, *Quellen*, 118–22.

39. Paravy, "À propos de la genèse," 334–35; Ostorero et al., *Imaginaire*, 273–74.
40. Ostorero et al., *Imaginaire*, 274.
41. Ibid., 107; Bailey, *Battling Demons*, 95–96, 153.

referred to as "vauderie." It was, therefore, originally dated to around 1460, subsequent to the more famous case of *vauderie* in the northern French city of Arras in 1459/60.[42] New manuscript discoveries have since been made, however, and in particular one copy of the text has been found that contains an addendum naming certain officials active in Lyon at the time of its composition. Their years of activity are at least approximately known, and when this information is combined with other scraps of evidence the text as a whole can now be dated most likely to the years 1439–41, allowing it to join the "first generation" of sources describing the witches' sabbath in the 1430s.[43]

42. Hansen, *Quellen*, 188. On witchcraft in Arras, see Andrew Colin Gow, Robert B. Desjardins, and François V. Pageau, *The Arras Witch Treatises* (University Park: Pennsylvania State University Press, 2016).

43. Franck Mercier and Martine Ostorero, *L'énigme de la Vauderie de Lyon: Enquête sur l'essor de la chasse aux sorcières entre France et Empire (1430–1480)* (Florence: SISMEL, 2015), 195–97.

Report on Witchcraft in Valais

HANS FRÜND

Hans Fründ was born in Lucerne around the beginning of the fifteenth century. He became a civic official and served as chief clerk of the canton of Schwyz from 1437 until 1461. He died in Lucerne probably in 1468. His most famous work was his chronicle of the Old Zurich War, waged between Zurich and the other Swiss cantons, covering the years 1436 until 1447 (the war itself lasted from 1440 to 1446).

His brief account of witchcraft in the region of Valais is contained in a manuscript consisting of various historical and juridical texts, now found in Lucerne's central library. Valais, to the south of Lucerne, was not yet part of the Swiss Confederation at this time, and it was divided both politically and linguistically. All of Valais lay in the diocese of Sion, its major and central city. The western or "lower" part of Valais, however, which was French speaking, was under the political control of the dukes of Savoy, whose territories stretched down into northwestern Italy. In the eastern or "upper" part of Valais, which was mainly German speaking, the bishop of Sion held nominal political as well as religious power, but in fact this area consisted of many fiercely independent lordships and communities.

The trials described by Fründ broke out in 1428. He wrote his report after they had been underway for about a year and a half. At one point, he described more than one hundred people having been executed, and shortly thereafter he raised this number to more than two hundred. Moreover, as he noted, witches were "still being convicted and burned every day." In fact, this wave of witch trials in Valais lasted until at least 1436, and other records have been discovered that corroborate Fründ's report.[1] Based on those, an estimate

---

1. Chantal Ammann-Dobliez, "La première chasse aux sorciers en Valais (1428–1436?)," in Ostorero et al., *Imaginaire*, 63–98.

of around one hundred executions across the entire region does not seem improbable.[2]

Some of the unique details in Fründ's report are also confirmed by these records, at least to the extent that they appear in the (perhaps coerced) testimonies of accused witches. For example, Fründ's is the only source translated here that mentions witches transforming, or believing themselves to transform, into wolves. Trial records from Valais report witches both supposedly transforming into wolves and, in another case, riding on a wolf.[3] There appears to be no discussion of flying to a sabbath in the surviving trial records from the 1430s, but the unique form of flight that Fründ described, on a chair covered with magical ointment rather than on a broom or staff, does appear in later trial records from this region.[4]

That Fründ's report was of more than just local interest is confirmed by the fact that a second copy has been found, now held in Strasbourg.[5] It is a later version in which certain details have been added or expanded. Most likely it represents part of the diffusion of early ideas about conspiratorial witchcraft and the sabbath from regions immediately surrounding the western Alps to the rest of Western Europe.

The two known manuscript copies of Fründ's report are now found in Lucerne and Strasbourg.[6] Joseph Hansen first edited the Lucerne copy in 1901 but got major sections of the text out of order. I have used the superior edition by Kathrin Utz Tremp in *L'imaginaire du sabbat*.[7] Not long after Hansen, Theodor von Liebenau published what appeared to be a later variant of the report.[8] The source of that

---

2. Ostorero et al., *Imaginaire*, 86.

3. Ibid., 87.

4. Ibid., 89n96.

5. Georg Modestin, "'Von der hexen, so in Wallis verbrant wurdent': Eine wieder entdeckte Handschrift mit dem Bericht des Chronisten Hans Fründ über eine Hexenverfolgung im Wallis (1428)," *Vallesia* 60 (2005): 399–409.

6. Lucerne, Zentralbibliothek, MS BB 335 fol., cols. 483a–488b; Strasbourg, Bibliothèque nationale et

universitaire, MS 2.935 (formerly All. 727), fols. 162r–164r.

7. Hansen, *Quellen*, 533–37. Ostorero et al., *Imaginaire*, 30–45, along with French translation by Catherine Chène. On the issue of misordering, see Ostorero et al., *Imaginaire*, 27.

8. Von Liebenau, "Von der Hexen, so in Wallis verbrannt wurdent in den Tagen, do Cristofel von Silinen herr und richter was," *Anzeiger für Schweizerische Geschichte* n.s. 9 (1903): 135–38;

edition, however, was not clear. Only in 2005 did Georg Modestin discover and edit a version of the report from Strasbourg matching von Liebenau's. Here I will refer to the Strasbourg version only where it significantly departs from or adds to our understanding of the earlier Lucerne version. A previous full English translation is available.[9]

REPORT ON WITCHCRAFT IN VALAIS

Janchers, judge in Valais[10]
In the year 1428 counted from the birth of Christ, there appeared in the territory and diocese of Valais the wickedness, murder[ousness], and heresy of witches and sorcerers,[11] both women and men, who are called *sortileii* in Latin. And they were first found in two valleys in Valais, one of which is called Enffis and the other is called Urens,[12] and many were judged and burned. Then in the same year many were found in this same territory of Valais, at first especially among the French speakers, and then among the Germans, and also many people who belonged to the diocese of Valais who were under the authority of the Duke of Savoy.[13] And many have admitted to great wickedness and many murders and heretical beliefs and many wicked things, and they have confessed and also committed that which is called *sortileia* in Latin. And many of these things are described hereafter, but many

reprinted in Ostorero et al., *Imaginaire*, 47–51.

9. P. G. Maxwell-Stuart, *Witch Beliefs and Witch Trials in the Middle Ages: Documents and Readings* (London: Continuum, 2011), 184–87.

10. The Strasbourg copy has a more descriptive opening line: "About the witches that were burned in Valais in the days when Cristofel of Silinen was lord and judge." Christopher of Silenen was castellan of Sierre, located about ten miles east of Sion at the mouth of the valley of Anniviers (see note 12 below), in 1428. It has been suggested that "Janchers" might refer

to his relative, Heinzmann of Silenen, who was bailiff of Valais in 1427–28. This, however, is far from certain. See Ostorero et al., *Imaginaire*, 31, 90–92.

11. *der hexssen und der zuobern*; Fründ's text is the only one presented here originally written in a vernacular language rather than in Latin.

12. The valley of Hérens rises into the Alps from the Rhone River valley at Sion. The valley of Anniviers (German: Einfischtal) lies a few miles to the east.

13. See the introduction immediately above for details about the political and linguistic divisions in Valais at this time.

things will also remain concealed, so that no one will be made wicked through them.

In particular one should know that these people, both women and men, were guilty of these same acts and wickedness, and had acted and carried on as they had learned from the evil spirit. And when he knows that people are weak in holy Christian faith and are careless, then he tempts people and makes them understand that he will make them rich and powerful, and thereby give them the means so that they can avenge harm done to them, and punish the people who have made them suffer and force them to atone. And with such wicked deceptions he wins these people over through pride, greed, envy, hatred, and the enmity that a person bears against his or her neighbors. And then the evil spirit overcomes the people who are inclined to such things and do not live in fear of God, and he won over many in the aforesaid region who took up wicked ways, as stated above.

And before he was willing to teach them these things, they had to commit themselves to the evil spirit and thereby deny God and all his saints, holy Christian baptism and the holy church, and enter into his service. And they had to pay him an annual tribute in various ways, namely, with a black sheep or lamb, another with a measure of oats, one with a part of his body after his death and with other services, as they had agreed with him and he with them, as they themselves later confessed. And the evil spirit appeared to them most often in the form of a black animal, sometimes in the form of a bear, sometimes in the form of a ram or in a terrible evil form, and spoke with them about wicked things, as described above.

And when he won them over, he forbade them to go to church either for Mass or for a sermon, and also that they should not confess these things to any priest, and that they would not go to confess to any priest what they had accomplished through their art, so that one could not prove it. And there were many of these people who, if they were arrested, could express themselves better than other uncouth people, and call upon God and his saints much more quickly than others, so that one took them to be innocent. And some of them did not confess at all, instead letting themselves be tortured to death before they would willingly confess or say anything. Some, however, confessed easily and felt great remorse about their sins.

Note:[14] They also confessed that they had given people poison and many harmful things to eat, many of whom died or became lame or very sick, and that the evil spirit taught them such wickedness and [ways of] killing, and gave them power, so that they could threaten and curse people who were in conflict with them or who angered them, so that some harm would immediately befall them. One became sick, another lame in his limbs, or became mad. Many were blinded. Many also lost their children because their wives gave birth at the wrong time. Also, many no longer wanted to sleep with their wives.[15] They also bewitched many women so that they became barren, and did many wicked things of this sort, about which they testified, and of which they were accused, and to which they themselves also confessed. And [there were] many other things to which they themselves confessed, about which no one knew anything up until that time.

Also [they confessed] how the evil spirit carried them at night from one mountain to another, and how he taught them to make ointments with which they would anoint chairs and then ride on them from one village to another and from one castle to another, and then gather in the cellars of the people who had the best wine. They enjoyed themselves there and afterward went wherever they wanted. And they were asked whether there was then somewhat less wine that they had drunk. They answered and said yes, there was less in the casks from which they had drunk, and the wine also became less good, because they put harmful materials in it that people did not notice.

There were also many among them whom the evil spirit taught to turn into wolves, so that they thought so themselves and did not know differently, only that they seemed to be wolves. And those who saw them at that time did not know differently, only that a man or a woman seemed to be a wolf at that moment. And they pursued sheep, lambs, and goats, and ate them raw in the guise of wolves. And when they wanted to, they became humans again, as [they were] before. The evil spirit also taught many of them that, by means of many herbs, they could cause themselves to become invisible so that no

---

14. This word is in Latin (*nota*) rather than German, and is marked in red ink in the original manuscript, drawing attention to this passage.

15. I.e., they became impotent.

one might see them. There were also many among them who could relieve injuries that other sorcerers[16] had inflicted on people, such as lameness or illness, and transfer it to other people and stir people up against each other.

There were also many among them who gathered together at schools in secret places.[17] Then the evil spirit arrived like a [school] master and preached to them against the Christian faith and forbade them confession and penance. And then they confessed to the master whether they had gone to church or what good deeds they had done, for which they received penance from the evil spirit, and many other evil articles that they then carried out, which ought not to be written down. There were also many among them who killed their own children and roasted and ate them, or boiled them and took them to their assembly and ate them.[18] And then they took decoys or other awful things that they had made to church,[19] and no one knew any different, only that they were children. Thus they left them [the real children] at home and ate them whenever they wanted. Many were also so wicked that they attacked their own children or other people's children at night and pressed them, and they would then waste away for several days and then die. Then they let their neighbors see them, and wherever they had touched them with their wicked hands, there the children were black or blue because of the evil poisonous material that they had spread on their hands. And they gave people to understand that the blessed souls had touched them,[20] and they acted sorrowfully around

16. *zoubrer.*

17. In this context, "schools" (*schuolen*) was another term for a heretical assembly.

18. The text literally reads "who killed their own children and roasted and ate and boiled them and took them to their assembly and ate them." The Strasbourg version clarifies this as "who killed their own children and roasted and boiled them, and then took them to their assembly and ate them there together."

19. *Und tragent den ludern oder ander boeß geschefft ze kilchen. Ludern* literally means "bait" or "lure," here

clearly in the sense of something made to appear to be something else. *Geschefft* means "creature" in the sense of a thing that has been fashioned or created. The Strasbourg copy adds a clarification: "And [they] lay decoys or other things in the little coffin and took them to church, as if they were their children."

20. The blessed souls (*die seligen selen*), or in other cases the blessed folk (*Säligen Lütt*), were spirit-creatures, often believed to be spirits of the dead. See Wolfgang Behringer, *Shaman of Obserstdorf: Chonrad Stoeckhlin and the Phantoms of the Night*, trans. H. C.

the children. And when they were buried, they went there at night and dug them up again and ate them in secret together.

And many of them confessed to such murders and wickedness, such as no Christians should rightly know, nor would one believe it had they not attested to it themselves. In fact, they themselves have provided such evidence showing that it is unfortunately true that they have often caused such harm. Also there are many who were not guilty of such great wickedness, heresy, and murders, but since they had performed other such wickedness and heresy and sorcery, they were also convicted and burned. There were also some among them who themselves confessed that they spoiled the fruit of the earth, especially wine and grain in the fields, with curses and other wickedness. And they maintained that they had power from the evil spirit so that they might do this, because they had given themselves to him. There were also some among them who took away people's milk, so that either their cows would not give milk or else their milk was not usable.[21] Some of them could also damage harnesses and ploughs so that they were of no use.

There were also many among them who neither wanted nor were able to confess, although there was much evidence against them, and others had denounced them who had all provided evidence. And they maintain that something had been done to them so that they could not confess about other witches.[22] And no matter how they were questioned with much harsh and severe torture, many of them never willingly confessed, and they let themselves be tortured so much that they died from it. Still, they were convicted and burned, some [already] dead and some [still] living.

The legal proceedings against these people lasted more than one and a half years, and more than one hundred people in the territory of Valais, both men and women, were burned after trial and judgment. And there were many who had practiced it [witchcraft] for nearly nine years, and some people who had learned and pursued it for a much

Erik Midelfort (Charlottesville: University of Virginia Press, 1998), 66–69; or Lecouteux, *Phantom Armies of the Night*, 155–59.

21. I.e., it was spoiled in some way.
22. The implication being that they themselves had been bewitched to keep them from confessing.

longer time had also given it up for many years and [then] had begun again nine years ago.

Note:[23] And there were so many of them that they thought, if they were able to remain at large for just one more year, they could have raised up a king from among them. And the evil spirit gave them to understand that they should become so strong that they should fear no political power or court of law, and that they themselves should set up a court and so constrain Christianity. And they also thought that if they got through the year in which they had been imprisoned,[24] then their [numbers] would increase even more, for there were already many of them. For they confessed that fully seven hundred were in their society, of which more than two hundred had been burned in one and a half years. And they are still being convicted and burned every day, whenever they can be caught. And many were also burned in the French-speaking territories and valleys of lower Valais and near Saint Bernhard's mountain,[25] although I do not know the full number, therefore I can neither write nor enumerate it. Only that they are thought to have grown so numerous because God wanted to make apparent their great wickedness and their unclean false beliefs, from which God protects all Christian people and firmly strengthens [our] faith and godly law, so that through these we will possess eternal life after this life. So help us God and Mary his mother, in the name of the Holy Trinity, that ever was and always will be to the end, amen. Amen.

He who wrote me was called Johannes Fründ.[26]

23. Again the word is in Latin (as note 14 above), here added in the margin of the text.

24. The Strasbourg copy modifies and adds to this: "And they thought that if they were not imprisoned this year, they would have become lord and master of the territory of Valais, and they would remain free in the territory of Valais for fifty years."

25. A reference to the Great St. Bernard Pass in lower Valais.

26. This line was added in Latin by another hand.

So That the Errors of Magicians and Witches . . .

CLAUDE THOLOSAN

Claude Tholosan was a native of the region of Dauphiné, in the south-east of France. He appears to have come from a family of lawyers. We know of an Antoine Tholosan who held a position as magistrate before him. After Claude obtained his degree in civil law, he served as chief magistrate in Briançon, a town high in the Alps southeast of Grenoble. The territory of Dauphiné had only been incorporated firmly into the kingdom of France less than a century before Tholosan was active, and in his role of chief magistrate, he played a major role in asserting royal power there.

Tholosan served in this post from 1426 until 1449. After about a decade of service, and after hearing more than one hundred cases of witchcraft, he decided to write a general account of this "execrable error and sect." Despite his own supposedly extensive experience with witches, the judge also gave some indication of just how new and strange the ideas he intended to relate were at this time, noting that he fully expected certain people to dismiss his accounts. Even though the evidence was right before their eyes, they would "disdain to see very obvious things," for they could only "think themselves learned if they disparage others." One can easily imagine in this the complaint of a member of a new elite, a man of somewhat rustic origins who had gone to university and gotten a good government job, and who was now about to report on strange and terrible crimes that more established elites continued to ignore.

In the first part of Tholosan's account, he offered a straightforward description of the activities of witches, especially as they gathered together in their diabolical assemblies. He noted how they swore loyalty to the devil and how they worked harm. They also healed people on occasion, although only to deceive them into thinking that their power could be beneficent. In fact, prior to Tholosan's rigorous investigation of their activities, many people had turned to them as soothsayers and to communicate with the spirits of the dead. In this small admission, we likely get a sense of what these "witches" really were—healers and diviners to whom people turned regularly, if perhaps somewhat nervously, for their extraordinary services.

Tholosan also presented witches as a foreign intrusion into the region around Briançon. Near the end of the first section of his account, he declared emphatically that these people had come to Briançon from Lombardy, to the east, and from Lyon, to the northwest. Closer to home, they had also come from the neighboring valley of Champsaur, about twenty-five miles southwest of Briançon as the crow flies (although that flight would have been over some fearsome mountain peaks).

Closing out this first, descriptive section of his account, Tholosan seems to have returned to the notion that people might not believe him, and so he presented a long list of legal, scriptural, and other authoritative citations about the power of magic and the devil. He then again referenced his personal experience with witches.[1]

This first section of *So That the Errors of Magicians and Witches . . .* represents less than a third of the overall text. The remainder becomes even more legalistic and technical. Tholosan's concern was to articulate exactly what kind of crimes witchcraft entailed, how those crimes should be punished, and most importantly by whom. The potential conflict here was between secular and ecclesiastical jurisdiction. Tholosan recognized that bishops and church inquisitors had some rightful jurisdiction over witches. Indeed, they were already operating against them in regions around Briançon. His main goal was therefore to delineate a clear role for secular justice as well.

As Tholosan wrote in the second section of his treatise, "the punishment which is owed to them [witches] is manifold, because the bishop . . . punishes them out of his ordinary power. . . . Also, an inquisitor involves himself when the deviancy smacks of manifest

---

1. Tholosan's modern editors (see note 5 below) include two more paragraphs in what they designate the first section of his treatise, but Tholosan was already turning there to matters that would concern him in the remaining sections of this work.

heresy . . . [and] secular authority involves itself in such matters in regard to the imposition of corporal punishment and the confiscation of goods."[2] He then provided a number of legal references to support this division of power, including quoting in full a letter from Peter of Blois, a twelfth-century theologian and canon lawyer. Peter had served in the chancery of Richard of Dover, the archbishop of Canterbury, just after the murder of the previous archbishop, Thomas Becket, at the behest of the English king Henry II. As such, he was well positioned to consider the intricacies of royal versus ecclesiastical power. Tholosan followed this in the third section of his treatise with an extensive contemporary legal opinion written primarily by Jordan Brice, the chief magistrate of Provence from 1420 until 1439.

In the final section of *So That the Errors of Magicians and Witches . . .* , Tholosan laid out his own rationale for the division of jurisdiction over witchcraft. First and foremost, since ecclesiastical courts could not impose the death penalty, they had to rely on secular courts to administer that punishment, and Tholosan was quick to assert that this did not entail a double punishment but rather simply one system of justice supporting and complementing another. He also argued strenuously, however, for independent secular jurisdiction over such cases. To do so, he equated witchcraft to treason against "divinity and humanity alike."[3] Here he drew on the power of the imperial *fisc* in Roman law, now equated with the power of the royal treasury. In antiquity this office had possessed, and so Tholosan argued that agents of the king now had, jurisdiction over the property and the lives of any traitor.

Tholosan's treatise thus developed into an important argument not only about the separation of church and state but also about emerging royal and national power in a legal world still defined by ancient Roman imperial laws. All of this is fascinating, but it makes for hard reading—a long slog through dense legalese. Moreover, although it is certainly important in terms of understanding the legal status of witchcraft as this time, it has little direct bearing on the idea of the witches' sabbath. Thus I have limited my translation to the first section of the text.

2. Ostorero et al., *Imaginaire*, 378.   3. Ibid., 402.

The only known copy of *So That the Errors of Magicians and Witches . . .* is found in Grenoble.[4] It was originally edited by Pierrette Paravy, and this edition was reprinted, along with a French translation by Martine Ostorero, in *L'imaginaire du sabbat.*[5] A German version of Paravy's introduction to the text, along with a German translation of the text itself (but not the original Latin edition), also exists.[6] Only highly abbreviated excerpts have previously been available in English.[7]

SO THAT THE ERRORS OF MAGICIANS AND WITCHES . . .

So that the errors of magicians and witches might be made evident to ignorant people, as Saint Augustine says in his book *The City of God*[8]—[errors] that, alas, have for a long time grown in great numbers, especially in all the lands of faithful Christians, as I well know—and especially after uniform and convincing testimony was confirmed by much evidence, I decided and undertook to present them in a general account in order to eradicate the execrable error and sect of these witches, and to this effect. Wherefore, following Jerome,[9] I do not doubt that there will be many who, through either envy or pride, would rather disdain to see very obvious things than to learn about them, and to drink from a very muddy stream rather than from the clearest spring, and what is more, that they think themselves learned if they disparage others. I, however, aware of my insignificance, will always recollect this knowledge: I said, I will guard my ways, so that I will not offend with my tongue. I have put a guard on my mouth,

---

4. Grenoble, Archives Départmentales de l'Isère, B 4356, fols. 69r–80r.

5. Paravy, "À propos de la genèse," 332–79; Ostorero et al., *Imaginaire,* 363–415.

6. Andreas Blauert, ed., *Ketzer, Zauberer, Hexen: Die Anfängen der europäischen Hexenverfolgungen* (Frankfurt: Suhrkamp, 1990), 118–59.

7. Kors and Peters, *Witchcraft in Europe,* 164–66.

8. This opening phrase echoes a passage from canon law (C. 26 q. 5 c. 14) which paraphrases Augustine. On legal citations, see note 24 below.

9. Jerome (ca. 347–420) was an early church father; the final clause of the following sentence ("they think themselves learned . . .") is from his commentary on Ephesians.

when a sinner stood facing me. I was speechless and humbled and kept silent about good things.[10]

First, following [the rules of] the sect and likewise the oath they have sworn to the devil, these witches, so called on account of the magnitude of their crimes,[11] as both laws testify,[12] must insofar as possible bring into the sect innocents whom, by the revelation of the devil, they know are inclined to vengeance or sensual pleasures. They also promise not to expose or accuse each other, and if they do, the devil can destroy them, both their body and possessions, as well as those of their immediate family and more distant relations. And under this penalty, they must not reveal anything about themselves to ministers of the church or to priests, or even to the ministers of justice by whom they are pursued and delivered to ultimate punishment. In fact, at the devil's command, they would instead promise to let themselves be killed, and, as I truly learned, the devil sometimes protects and strengthens them during interrogations, so that they do not feel the torture, and he appears to them there, strengthening them.

Also, at their master's instigation, those entering this sect deny God, whom they call the prophet, and they completely withdraw from Christ's faith by overturning some vessel that they place in a circle that they have drawn in the dirt, in which the devil urinates, from which they drink and then return it [to the circle]. They also turn their hand or some other item backward, again denying the law of God and his faith entirely, not believing in the articles of faith or the sacraments of the church, turning their posteriors and naked ass to heaven as an insult to God, making a cross in the soil, spitting on it three times and trampling it with their foot in contempt of God, whom they call the prophet, as said, and making the fig three times against the prophet and toward the rising sun.[13]

Also, after this, in the same place and straight away, they kneel and kiss the devil, who usually appears to them in the form of a human being or of many different animals. And they kiss him on the mouth,

10. Psalm 38:2–3 (medieval Vulgate) / 39:1–2 (Hebrew numbering).

11. Recall that the Latin term for witches, *malefici*, literally meant "evil-doers" or criminals.

12. I.e., civil and canon law.

13. An obscene hand gesture.

giving him their body and soul, along with one of their children, most often their firstborn, whom they sacrifice and offer to him on their knees, holding the naked [child] under the arms and shoulders. Finally, they kill it and exhume it after burial, and from it, along with other things described below, they make a powder. And he [the devil] is seen to appear according to the desire of the person being subjected to him, so that if that person is wanton and young, [he appears] in a beautiful form. They make an annual tribute to him, in the aforesaid way, on the day when they [first] subjugated themselves. It pleases them that he appears to them thus, that they might have business with him,[14] whom they declare to be cold as ice. They also declare that his body, like glass, does not block the rays of the sun. He forbids to them all faith and belief in the rites of the church, which the devil fears. And he promises to deliver them from their enemies and to protect them, although not to free them from the hands of justice, unless they conceal the detestable crimes they have committed. And he tells them that he cannot harm ministers of justice.

Moreover, he gives himself whatever name he wants, with the surname "devil," presaging to them that he is the devil of hell, and all-powerful, and a god. He enjoins them to all base things, especially to pleasures of the flesh and wantonness. He persuades them that they should feign devotion without faith, attending church, which they do for the most part. And in whatever relief they provide,[15] they should feign something good but partly superstitious. And they relieve many troubled people from this kind of malady,[16] on account of which relief they say that previously, before such an investigation as this, people called upon them as soothsayers and they received responses from the dead.

Also, he deludes them in dreams, such that they believe that they journey physically during the night, especially on Thursdays and Saturdays, with a troop of devils to strangle children and to inflict infirmities, drawing the fat out of the children, whom they boil and eat there. And they go to one particular place, where they hold a

---

14. I.e., sexual intercourse.

15. I.e., magical healing.

16. What malady or sickness Tholosan means is unclear. The people

afflicted are described as *anxiatos*, meaning troubled, worried, or in anguish.

synagogue for the region. They also carry a pennant on which there is the figure of the chief devil, to whom, as is said below, they report on [their] witchcraft and present new [members] of the sect. And they declare that they travel far, some on a staff anointed with children's fat and the powder described below along with the devil's urine, and some on beasts and brooms. They hold a synagogue, kiss the devil, and at his command have carnal knowledge of each other, and they mingle with demons, sometimes even against nature,[17] and they return in an instant. They also think that they eat and drink in houses that the devils open, and perform all kinds of wicked things, and sometimes they dance to the sound of an instrument with the devil's troop, as is described concerning Saul in 1 Kings 16[:23], where the wicked spirit was stilled by the sound of the harp.[18] These faithless people even think that they sometimes eat and drink there, diminishing [the food and drink]. And a greater devil is there, the chief of the region, sitting on a throne, to whom they pay reverence, and they give a report about the wicked things they have done, and they consider doing worse things by making powders there.

Also, they prepare poisonous powders from poison that they buy from apothecaries, along with the devil's urine and many other poisons, and with the aid of the devil they give it to their enemies. This powder is administered through magical trickery,[19] so that they are invisible while administering it, even in a mirror, secretly and with the devil's aid. And based on the amount, [this powder] causes illness or sudden death, without [any possible] cure by physicians, sometimes even appearing as an ulcer.

Also, with a long thistle and the devil's urine, a cock's egg,[20] and certain other things they hinder conception in women and they render people mad. And with menstrual blood, at the touch of which trees are desiccated, and also with chrism, they drive people to lust and love of sensual pleasure, with the aid of the devil. They also perform witchcraft with the sacrament of the altar and the body of the Lord,

---

17. I.e., homosexually.

18. 1 Kings in the medieval Vulgate is now more commonly designated 1 Samuel.

19. *prestigiose.*

20. Small, usually yokeless eggs traditionally believed to be lain by roosters and often thought to hatch cockatrices.

and with wax [made] from the fat of a child, especially one strangled before being baptized. They call a child who has died thus a virgin. And with the aforesaid powder they make an image. By pricking it they torment and mistreat whomever they want, or rather by striking it with a twisted stick or a cord onto which the devil spits. And the witches strike it, saying "I chew you,"[21] and the devil says to them that he will hasten to afflict them,[22] which must not be made known to everyone. And sometimes, when divine judgment permits, with the aid of the devil they hinder marriages, and the devil tells them that he takes away the strength and ardor of a person having sex, especially, as I learned, from people without faith and those who are lustful as the horse and the mule, as is read in Tobias.[23]

Also, they kill people by touching a piece of their clothing and in many other ways, with the aid of the devil, and they reveal many secrets, and they inflict infirmities and heal many people in accordance with this [legal principle]: The mind of one consumed by no bloody drought of poison perishes through spells, as [stated in Case] 25, question 5, canon *Nimirum*.[24] They also say that, although the devil may appear in human form and be palpable, nevertheless he casts no shadow when facing the sun, nor is he seen except by whom he wishes.

Know that the authors of these [crimes] came from Lombardy in the guise of physicians, from Lyon as ruffians and pimps, [and] from Champsaur as beggars and soothsayers,[25] uniformly holding and belonging to the aforesaid execrable sect.

No wonder that such things should occur, caused by faithlessness and temptation, even to innocent people on account of their wavering, as is read in [Case] 26, question 5, especially in the canons *Contra*

---

21. Probably in the sense of "I am devouring you." In many cultures, affliction by witchcraft is described in terms of being eaten or devoured by a witch.

22. I.e., the people depicted by the image.

23. Tobit 6:17.

24. A reference to canon law, specifically to the so-called *Decretum*, dating to ca. 1140 and traditionally attributed to the Bolognan legal scholar Gratian. This section of the *Decretum* is standardly cited according to its subdivisions of Case, question, and canon. Tholosan gets the Case number wrong; the correct citation is C. 26 q. 5 c. 14. The quote itself comes from Lucan's *Civil War*, book 6.

25. A valley in the Alps south of Grenoble.

ydolorum, Episcopi, [and] *Nimirum;*[26] also throughout the whole [title] *De maleficiis et mathematicis* in the Code;[27] in the Institutes, *De publicis judiciis;*[28] in the Old [Compilations], *De frigidis et maleficiatis,* and generally [as described] by theologians and teachers in *De sortilegiis;*[29] by Isidore in the book that he wrote, *De summo bono,* in the title *De angelis;*[30] in the Bible in Genesis, about the serpent;[31] in Exodus, about witches opposing Moses;[32] and in Leviticus, Numbers, and Deuteronomy; in the commandments and prohibitions; and also in Joshua; First Kings, about Saul and the diviner, and how an evil angel troubled him;[33] and Fourth Kings; and Second Paralipomenon, about Ahaz and Manasseh and many others doing similar things;[34] [and] how David was punished through his children, and his sin was turned back on his son and brought [him] to death;[35] in Tobias, about Sarah's husbands being strangled by the devil;[36] in Job, about the killing of his children and the violence of the elements, in order to test him;[37] and generally in the entire Old and New Testament; and especially about Jesus carried off and tempted by the devil appearing in human form;[38] and Paul buffeted by the devil, who also says: the angel Satan transforms himself into an angel of light;[39] and Peter the Apostle: your

26. Again canon law citations from the *Decretum:* C. 26 q. 5 c. 10, 12, 14.

27. The Code was a standard work of Roman civil law, first issued by the Byzantine emperor Justinian (r. 527–65); here Cod. 9.18.

28. Another Roman civil law collection issued by Justinian; here Inst. 4.18.

29. The Five Old Compilations (*Quinque compilationes antiquae*) were legal collections mostly incorporated into the first major expansion of canon law after the *Decretum,* known as the *Liber extra,* issued by Pope Gregory IX in 1234. The standard modern citation form begins with X (for Extra) followed by numbers indicating book, title, and chapter. Here, however, Tholosan refers to entire titles, not specific chapters: X 4.15, X 5.21.

30. Isidore of Seville (ca. 560–636), actually his *Sententiae* 1.10.

31. Genesis 3:1–5.

32. Exodus 7–8, describing Moses and Aaron's contest of power with Pharaoh's court magicians (called *malefici* in the Vulgate).

33. 1 Kings (1 Samuel) 16:14–23, in which Saul is troubled by an evil spirit; 1 Kings (1 Samuel) 28:7–25, in which he visits a female diviner later known as the "witch" of Endor.

34. In 2 Paralipomenon (2 Chronicles) 28 and 33, the Hebrew kings Ahaz and Manasseh worship idols.

35. In 2 Kings (2 Samuel) 12:11–19, God afflicts King David's household, killing his son.

36. Tobit 3:8 and 6:14 relate how the demon Asmodeus killed seven of Sarah's husbands.

37. Job 1:19, in which a violent wind collapses a house, killing Job's children.

38. Jesus's temptation in the desert: Matt. 4:1–11, Mark 1:12–13, Luke 4:1–13.

39. 2 Corinthians 11:14, 12:7.

adversary the devil goes around seeing whom he might devour; resist him, strong in faith;[40] and in the lives of saints Germanus, Francis, Anthony, Martin, Cyprian and Justine, Basil, and many others; and also in the Acts of the Apostles [where] one reads about Paul opposing a Roman witch.[41] Likewise it is demonstrated in the *Summa* of Serva-sanctus, [where] he writes about the devil's activities and deceptions, and as it says: [When] God is angry at this world by whatever scourge, they are sent to administer punishment by an apostate angel.[42] They are nevertheless restrained by divine power, so that they cannot do as much harm as they wish. I learned the same through the account of witches, to whom sometimes demons reported that they could not harm those against whom they were sent, using this expression: that they were armed with the inestimable armor of the prophet.[43] And for the sake of brevity, these few [examples] set out above should suffice.

And the things set out above I, Claude Tholosan, licensed in law, chief magistrate of Dauphiné in Briançon, learned from experience through the accounts of witches, alas, more than a hundred in number, by lawful means of information, and also from people bewitched by them.

---

40. 1 Peter 5:8–9.

41. Although Tholosan writes here of a female witch (*malefica*), this must refer to Paul's confrontation with the Jewish magician Bar-Jesu, a.k.a. Elymas, in Acts 13:6–11. The Vulgate does not, in fact, label Elymas a witch (*maleficus*) but a magician (*magus*).

42. Servasanctus of Faenza, an Italian Franciscan of the thirteenth century. The grammar is slightly gar-bled, but the passage is originally from Isidore of Seville, *Sententiae* 1.10.18 (the title *De angelis*, see note 30 above), where it reads more clearly: "Whenever God, by whatever scourge, is angry at this world, apostate angels are sent to administer punishment."

43. I.e., Jesus.

Errors of the Gazarii

ANONYMOUS

The *Errors of the Gazarii*[1] is a brief source that presents extremely graphic and lurid descriptions of a witches' sect and sabbath. Since it provides little else, however, scholars have faced a challenge situating it securely in its proper historical context. The text was long thought to date to around 1450, and its author was assumed to be an inquisitor, probably operating in Savoy.[2] Only the discovery of a second version of the tract allowed it to be redated to the 1430s.[3] The longer of these two versions included a description of witches harvesting ice from mountaintops to produce hail that closely resembled testimony from a trial conducted by the Dominican inquisitor Ulric de Torrente in Lausanne. One scholar therefore subsequently suggested that it was "not unlikely" that the tract was composed in that area.[4] Closer study, however, suggests that the tract was originally written in the northwestern corner of Italy, in the region of Aosta. The most likely candidate to be its author was a Franciscan inquisitor, Ponce Feugeyron.[5]

Wherever it was composed, the *Errors of the Gazarii* echoed and often amplified elements of conspiratorial witchcraft and the sabbath that were developing at this time. In one possible connection, Ponce Feugeyron briefly attended the Council of Basel in 1433, where he might well have met Johannes Nider. Nider did not mention Feugeyron in his *Anthill*, but that is not surprising since Feugeyron had not yet

---

1. A generic term for heretics or malefactors.

2. Hansen, *Quellen*, 118.

3. Paravy, "À propos de la genèse," 333; Ostorero et al., *Imaginaire*, 358, 417.

4. Andreas Blauert, *Frühe Hexenverfolgungen: Ketzer-, Zauberei- und Hexenprozesse des 15. Jahrhunderts* (Hamburg: Junius, 1989), 62–63.

5. Ostorero et al., *Imaginaire*, 330–34; Martine Ostorero, "Itinéraire d'un inquisiteur gâté: Ponce Feugeyron, les Juifs et le sabbat des sorciers," *Médiévales* 43 (2002): 103–18; Ostorero, *Diable au sabbat*, 33–39.

conducted any witch trials himself. He began to do so only in 1434, after he had left the council. Hence he could not have presented Nider any firsthand information about witchcraft, but they still might have discussed the issue, which was soon to be of interest to them both. Clearly the *Errors of the Gazarii* had some kind of association with the Council of Basel, because both early copies of the text are found in manuscripts that contain sources relating to the council.[6]

In structure, the *Errors* is most like the substantially longer *Vauderie of Lyon*, perhaps not surprising given that both were written by inquisitors. It recounts horrific elements of witchcraft and the sabbath in quick succession, and it actually provides more detail on certain points than do some considerably longer sources. It gives the fullest account, for example, of why people might choose to enter the witches' sect, owing to greed, desire for power, or carnal lust. It also gives the most detailed description found in any of these texts of witches performing weather magic. And of course, if one is looking for an account of exactly how to distill poisons from the corpse of a redheaded man, then the *Errors of the Gazarii* is really one's only option.

There are now three known manuscript copies of the *Errors*. Scholars were first aware of the version now held in the library of the University of Basel.[7] Then a second copy was discovered in the Vatican Library in Rome.[8] This copy is shorter and appears to have been written earlier than the Basel copy, which expands on it considerably. A third copy was subsequently found, also in the Vatican.[9] It mainly reproduces the Basel copy, and its transcription in the territories of the German Palatinate in the mid-1450s speaks to the rapid diffusion of the idea of the sabbath.

Joseph Hansen originally edited the Basel copy, whereas Kathrin Utz Tremp and Martine Ostorero edited both the Basel copy and earlier Vatican one in *L'imaginaire du sabbat*.[10] Ostorero subsequently

6. On other connections related to witchcraft at the Council of Basel, see Michael D. Bailey and Edward Peters, "A Sabbat of Demonologists: Basel, 1431–1440," *The Historian* 65 (2003): 1375–95.

7. Basel, Universitätsbibliothek, MS A II 34, fols. 319r–320v.

8. Rome, Biblioteca Apostolica Vaticana, MS Vat. Lat. 456, fols. 205v–206r.

9. Rome, Biblioteca Apostolica Vaticana, MS Pal. Lat. 1381, fols. 190r–192r.

10. Hansen, *Quellen*, 118–22; Ostorero et al., *Imaginaire*, 278–87,

produced a comparative edition of the Basel and Vatican-Palatinate texts.[11] Here I have translated the Basel version of the text, noting only where it varies significantly from, rather than just adding to, the earlier Vatican version. Two previous English translations are also available.[12]

THE ERRORS OF THE GAZARII, OR THOSE WHO ARE PROVEN TO RIDE ON A BROOM OR STAFF

First, when some person of either sex is seduced by someone, urged on by the enemy of human nature, the seducer, casting the seduced person into an abyss of evils, makes him swear that whenever he should demand it, the seduced person will hasten with him to the synagogue, leaving all other things aside, bearing in mind that the aforesaid seducer had to supply him with unguents appropriate for this, and a broom, which he does.

Also, when they are at the synagogue, the seducer strives to present the seduced person to the devil, the enemy of rational creatures. That enemy appears sometimes in the form of a black cat, sometimes in the form of a human being, although imperfect somehow, or in the guise of another animal, but most commonly in the guise of a black cat. When the seduced person is asked by the devil whether he wants to remain and continue in this fellowship, at a nod from his seducer he responds "yes." Hearing this, the devil requires an oath of fidelity from the seduced person, in the following manner. First he swears that he will be faithful to the presiding master and the whole fellowship. Second, that he will bring into the fellowship all those whom he can, insofar as it is possible. Third, that he will not reveal the secrets of the aforesaid sect, even unto death. Fourth, that he will strangle and kill all the children he can and bring them to the synagogue, and it is understood that these should be children of three years or younger.

along with a comparative edition and a French translation on pages 288–98.

11. Martine Ostorero and Kathrin Utz Tremp, with Georg Modestin, *Inquisition et sorcellerie en Suisse romande: Le register Ac 29 des Archives cantonales vaudoises (1438–1528)* (Lausanne: Université de Lausanne, 2007), 493–504.

12. Kors and Peters, *Witchcraft in Europe*, 160–62. Maxwell-Stuart, *Witch Beliefs and Witch Trials*, 70–74.

Fifth, that whenever he should be called to the synagogue, he will set everything else aside and hasten to come. Sixth, that he will impede all marriages, insofar as possible, through sorcery and other witchcraft.[13] Seventh, that he will avenge wrongs done to the sect or to any of its members, collectively or individually.

Having sworn and promised these things, the poor seduced person worships the presiding figure and pays homage to him. And as a sign of homage, he kisses the devil—appearing, as set out above, either in a human or in another form—on the ass or anus, granting him as a sign of tribute one of the limbs of his body after death. When these things are done, all the members of that pestiferous sect celebrate the arrival of the new heretic, eating whatever they have with them, especially children who have been killed, roasted, and boiled. And once this exceedingly wicked banquet is done, after they have danced as much as they wish, the presiding devil then calls out "*mestlet, mestlet*,"[14] while extinguishing the light. After they hear his voice, they join together carnally, man with woman, or man with man, and sometimes father with daughter, son with mother, brother with sister, and with the proper order of nature scarcely being observed. When these impious, extremely wicked, and irregular things are over, the light is relit and they eat and drink again, and while departing they urinate into [wine] casks, into which they also put course matter.[15] When asked why they do this, they say that they do it in contempt of the sacrament of the Eucharist and equally in disdain for what is consecrated by the wine. After these things are done, each returns to his home.

Also, after the seduced person pays homage to the presiding devil, he [the devil] gives to him a small box full of unguent and a staff and everything else that the seduced person needs to go to the synagogue, and he teaches him how he must anoint the staff. For that unguent is made through diabolical malignancy from the fat of roasted and boiled children, along with certain other things, as will be made clear.

Also, another unguent is made from the aforesaid fat of children mixed with extremely poisonous animals, for example serpents, toads,

---

13. *per sortilegia et alia maleficia.*
14. Perhaps related to the French verb *mêlez*, meaning roughly in this context "mix it up!" See Ostorero et al., *Imaginaire*, 291n2.
15. I.e., excrement.

lizards, [and] spiders, which are all mixed together with the aid of the devil. If someone should be touched once by this unguent, he will inevitably suffer a bad death, sometimes lingering for a long time in a feeble condition, sometimes dying suddenly.

Note about the officiality of Vevey and many others.[16]

Also, they make powders to kill people. That is, they make powders from children's innards mixed with the aforesaid poisonous animals. They scatter all of this, ground into a powder by one of the fellowship, through the air on a cloudy day, and those touched by this powder either die or suffer serious and persistent infirmity. And this is the reason that there is [so much] death in some towns and villages in one region, and in surrounding areas there is extremely inclement weather.[17]

Also, when these noxious people are able to get a redheaded person who is not from their sect, but a faithful Catholic, they strip him naked, binding him on a bench such that he is unable to move his hands or other limbs. Once bound, they surround him with poisonous animals, which are made to bite him all over by some especially merciless and cruel people from this sect, so that the poor person perishes in these torments and dies suffocated by poison. When dead, they hang him by his feet, placing under his mouth a glass or earthenware vessel to collect the impurities and poison dripping out of the person's mouth and other orifices. After collecting this, with the aid of the devil they make another unguent from the fat of those hanged on gibbets and the innards of children and the aforesaid poisonous animals, which kills all people at a single touch.

Also, with the aid of the devil they take the skin of a single cat and fill it with pulses, namely with barley, wheat, oats, [and] grapes, and they put the filled skin in an active wellspring and keep it there

16. *Nota de officialatu Viviaci*, referring to a municipal office in Vevey. See Martine Ostorero, *"Folâtrer avec les démons": Sabbat et chasse aux sorciers à Vevey (1448)* (Lausanne: Université de Lausanne, 1995), 45n46. This line is inserted between these two sections of text in the Basel copy. It is absent from the earlier Vatican copy.

Hansen, *Quellen*, 120n1, suggests it refers to witch trials in the region of Vevey, possibly including the trial of Aymonet Maugetaz, translated in this volume.

17. The Vatican copy reads simply "and because of this there is death in one region and not in another."

for three days.[18] Then, after taking these and drying them out, they grind them into a powder and, climbing up a mountain on a windy day, they scatter them on and around fertile regions and properties, and they say this causes sterility, and that, because of this sacrifice, the devil devours the fruits of the land over which they have spread the said powder.

Also, some of the sect, already burned [to death], have confessed that, at the command of the devil, many gathered in the mountains on stormy days in order to break off ice, and often great piles of ice were found in the mountains. They even say that some—but not all, because not all have the strength or boldness to do this—carry the ice, with the aid of the devil, through the air on stormy days, by means of a staff, in order to destroy the fertile holdings of their enemies and those around them.[19]

Also, according to the testimony of some or indeed all of them, all those from that sect who enter that damned fellowship generally enter for three reasons. First, because there are some who cannot live in peace, accumulating many enemies, their hand raised against all and all against them, being from the race of Ishmael.[20] Seeing that they cannot achieve vengeance on their enemies by human means, they ask to be avenged by the devil. Indeed, because the devil is accustomed to seduce simple people through their credulity, he often introduces the aforesaid error into their minds through fantasies, urging some of the sect to approach them in a neighborly way, in order to deceive and seduce them, giving this deception effective force. Approaching someone in order to console him, so they say, and dissembling, they will ask the cause of his sorrow, and in accordance with the different causes, they cast him down in various ways into a pit of sins, and, promising vengeance, they induce and persuade him to enter their fellowship,

---

18. Barley, wheat, oats, and grapes are not generally considered pulses. The intention may be to refer to the seeds of these plants.

19. This paragraph is absent from the earlier Vatican copy.

20. The biblical figure of Ishmael was the patriarch Abraham's first son, by his servant Hagar. After the birth of Abraham's son Isaac, by his wife Sarah, Abraham banished Hagar and Ishmael. In medieval Christian tradition, Ishmael's progeny were generally regarded as wicked outcasts from society.

promising moreover to give him the means of living freely and magnificently. To whatever they hear, they immediately offer assent.[21]

Also, there are some who are accustomed to live luxuriously, and living thus they consume all their goods, and others who want constantly to eat delicacies. Concerning them, the devil encourages some from the sect to bring them along to the synagogue, after informing them about the ceremonies of the sect pertaining to their desires. After this, at a prescribed time the devil leads them to the homes of powerful prelates, nobles, burghers, and others, in which he knows there is food and wine matching their wishes and desires, opening the cellars of the aforesaid powerful people to them around the third hour of the night and leading them in. And they remain there until the middle of the night or thereabouts, but not beyond this, because this is their hour and the dominion of darkness. After they have eaten and drunk sufficiently, each one returns to his own business.

Also, the third cause on account of which they enter that damned fellowship is because there are some who want to take pleasure wantonly in the sexual act, and because there they [can] lustfully follow [their] inclination as they will, therefore etc.[22]

Also, it is noted that the devil forbids anyone from the sect to steal gold and silver or precious vessels, lest the sect should be revealed because of the number and value of these things.

Also, they confess that when someone acts against the rules of the sect, by order of the master he is soundly whipped at night by someone from the fellowship, and because of this they are extraordinarily afraid of offending the master or their confederates in the sect.

Also, according to the confession of John of Etroubles[23] and others who have been burned, when one enters that sect for the first time, after offering the oath of fidelity and paying homage, as said above, the devil draws blood from the seduced person's left hand with a certain

21. This paragraph is significantly shorter in the earlier Vatican copy.

22. The earlier Vatican copy states more concisely: "Also, some even enter in order to fulfill their [carnal] desire, which they can pursue there as they will." The later Vatican (Pal. Lat.) copy reads: "And this is done because there are some who want to take pleasure wantonly in the sexual act, and because there they [can] lustfully follow [their] inclination as they will."

23. A town in the mountains north of the Italian city of Aosta.

instrument, and with this blood writes certain things on a parchment, which he then keeps with him, and many from the sect have seen this, as they have testified.

Also, wanting to strangle children when their father and mother are asleep, in the silence of the dead of night they enter the parents' house with the aid of the devil. Taking the child by the throat or by its sides, they press it until it is dead. And in the morning, when it is carried to the grave, he or she or they[24] who strangled and killed the child join in with others, and they mourn the death of the child along with its parents and friends. But the next night they open the grave[25] and take the child, sometimes leaving the child's head and hands and feet in the grave, for unless they want to perform some sorcery with the child's hand, they never take it with them. After this is done and the grave is refilled, they carry the child to the synagogue, where it is roasted and eaten, as has already been described.

And note that there are some who slay their own sons and daughters and eat them at the synagogue, such as Jeanne Vacanda, burned in a place called Chambave on Saint Lawrence's day.[26] And she acknowledged before all the people that she had eaten her son and daughter and had killed them with another woman named in her trial.

Also, it is evident from the confession of those who have been burned that those from the sect appear to be better than other faithful [Christians] and they generally attend Mass, confess often in a year, and frequently receive the holy Eucharist, just like Judas, who [received it] from the hand of the Lord, etc.,[27] and [they do] this lest, if they should draw back from receiving the sacrament, their error should be detected or exposed, etc.

24. The Basel copy is curiously specific here that the killer(s) might be one man, one woman, or a group. The earlier Vatican copy refers to "they" throughout this section.

25. The Basel copy uses *fovea*, literally meaning a small pit. The earlier Vatican copy states simply that "at night they dig it [the child] up," using the verb *effodiunt*.

26. August 10. *Chambanaz* (or *Chambanna* in the earlier Vatican copy) could refer to several places, but given the reference to Etroubles above, the most likely would be Chambave, a town about ten miles east of Aosta. For full discussion, see Ostorero et al., *Imaginaire*, 331.

27. The reference is to Judas sharing in the Last Supper and receiving bread from Christ. The earlier Vatican copy reads at this point "concealing his malice, etc."

Anthill

JOHANNES NIDER

Unlike the other authors translated here, who either remained anonymous or were important but decidedly local figures, Johannes Nider was a leading light within the Dominican order in his day, and important in the church as a whole. He was born in the early 1380s in the town of Isny, located in southern Germany just a few miles from what is now the Austrian border. He entered the Dominican order and was educated at the universities of Cologne and Vienna. He would later become dean of the theological faculty in Vienna. In between, he was a leader of the reform movement that was then very active within the Dominican order, and he served as prior of reformed Dominican convents first in Nuremberg and then in Basel. He was also an important figure during at least the first few years of the great ecumenical Council of Basel, which met from 1431 until 1449. Nider himself left the council probably in 1435 to return to Vienna. He died in Nuremberg in 1438.[1]

Nider wrote most if not all of his *Anthill* in Vienna, but he clearly collected much of his material on witchcraft while in Basel. His main sources of information, so he tells us, were a secular judge, Peter of Bern, and an unnamed Dominican inquisitor from Lyon.[2] He also heard about Joan of Arc, recently executed in northern France, from Nicolas Lami, a representative of the University of Paris to the Council of Basel.

The *Anthill* is a sprawling work addressing an array of topics. Even its fifth book, "On Witches and Their Deceptions," deals not just with witchcraft but also with demonic power, possession and exorcism,

1. See Bailey, *Battling Demons*; Werner Tschacher, *Der Formicarius des Johannes Nider von 1437/38: Studien zu den Anfängen der europäischen Hexenverfolgungen im Spätmittelalter* (Aachen: Shaker, 2000).

2. On these men, see notes 30 and 32 below.

dreams and visions, and various superstitious beliefs and folklore. The work took the form of a dialog between a Dominican theologian, who was clearly meant to be Nider himself, and a "lazy person" (*piger*) who was a young student in the order.[3] This format allowed Nider to introduce any topic he wanted, simply by having the lazy student ask about it. The theologian would typically respond first by citing biblical texts and scholastic theology. The student would then demand current examples, and it was here that Nider presented his accounts of contemporary witchcraft and the sabbath.

Because the *Anthill* is so much longer than the other works collected here, and because it draws on several different sources of information, it allows for interesting comparisons not only with those other works but also between its own different reports. For example, the *Anthill* appears to present both the newly developing notion of conspiratorial witchcraft and an older notion of witches acting more or less as individual malefactors. Nider certainly described witches operating as members of a sect, gathering together in the presence of a demon, placing themselves in its service, and engaging in various horrible rites. Interspersed with these accounts, however, he also discussed a single witch, a man named Scaedeli, who had been arrested and executed by Peter of Bern. Scaedeli clearly performed harmful witchcraft (that is, *maleficium*) with the aid of demons, but Nider never depicted him as belonging to a sect that gathered in large assemblies. He was associated with a few other witches, but only through personal connections. Scaedeli learned witchcraft, so Nider related, from a man named Hoppo, and the two of them clearly worked together for some period of time. Hoppo, in turn, had learned witchcraft from a man called Scavius.

Nider was also the first clerical writer to argue explicitly that women were more prone to witchcraft than were men, but I have already addressed that issue in the general introduction. Here let me just note how new and strange such an idea might have appeared to the educated clergymen who would have read the *Anthill*. Although

---

3. The term is from Proverbs 6:6,
"Go to the ant, O lazy one, and consider its ways and learn wisdom."

women had long been associated with many kinds of harmful magic, the form of demonic magic more familiar to most clergy in the early fifteenth century, especially those educated in schools and universities, would have been a variety of elite ritual magic known as necromancy.[4] Performed via complex rites and invocations read out of books, this type of magic was paradigmatically male. When the lazy student declared in *Anthill* 5.8, "I cannot wonder enough how the fragile sex dares to rush into such audacities," his declaration may have been more than a rhetorical trope. It might also have captured the real surprise many male elites could have felt at finding supposedly weak-willed and foolish women associated with demons, not as mere victims of possession but directing these creatures' terrible powers themselves.[5]

Whereas other texts translated here survive in just a few copies or are unique, Nider's *Anthill* exists in numerous manuscripts and seven early modern printed editions.[6] For *Anthill* 2.4, 5.3, 5.4, and 5.7, I have relied on the edition established by Catherine Chène in *L'imaginaire du sabbat*.[7] I have based the translation of *Anthill* 5.1 and 5.8 on the Cologne 1480 edition, which has been published in a lightly corrected modern form.[8] Because the work is so long, no complete translation exists. Brief excerpts can be found in several English-language source collections.[9]

4. See Richard Kieckhefer, *Magic in the Middle Ages* (Cambridge: Cambridge University Press, 1989), 151–75; Richard Kieckhefer, *Forbidden Rites: A Necromancer's Manual of the Fifteenth Century* (University Park: Pennsylvania State University Press, 1998).

5. An argument developed at greater length in Michael D. Bailey, "The Feminization of Magic and the Emerging Idea of the Female Witch in the Late Middle Ages," *Essays in Medieval Studies* 19 (2002): 120–34.

6. Ostorero et al., *Imaginaire*, 108–16.

7. Ibid., 122–99.

8. Jean Nider, *Des sorcieres et leurs trumperies:* La Fourmilière *Livre V*, ed. and trans. Jean Céard (Grenoble: Millon, 2005).

9. Kors and Peters, *Witchcraft in Europe*, 156–59; Maxwell-Stuart, *Witch Beliefs and Witch Trials*, 61–63; Brian P. Levack, *The Witchcraft Sourcebook*, 2nd ed. (London: Routledge, 2015), 55–57; Martha Rampton, *European Magic and Witchcraft: A Reader* (Toronto: University of Toronto Press, 2018), 282–86.

ANTHILL

Book 2, Chapter 4: Concerning different kinds of dreams, their causes, and those deceived by dreams and visions.

Deprived of sight, ants blunder along paths clear to others. For they waver then and do not know in which direction they are going. In effect, the same thing occurs to a reasoning person's mental "eyes." If deprived of the light of divine grace or the use of reason, a person is more like a beast or drunkard, in terms of morals, than a rational creature or angelic being, although in the beginning he was made and created [to be] scarcely less than this. The wise man hints at this danger of mental blindness and need for divine guidance in visions and dreams when, after offering some words about dreams, immediately he adds this: Just as the heart of a woman in labor, yours suffers from fantasies, unless the vision was sent from the Most High.[10] And Job 32[:8]: A spirit is in men and the inspiration of the Almighty gives understanding.

Lazy Student: Please teach [me] first how many different kinds of dreams there are. Then go on [to explain] the means of discerning the true from the false, so that we may know that we ought to beware or abide, lest along the narrow path of this dangerous valley we should deviate from the way of truth.

The theologian presents a long explanation of different kinds of dreams and their causes, beginning with biblical examples but drawing mainly on the thirteenth-century Dominican theologian Thomas Aquinas's analysis of dreams in his Summa theologiae *(2.2.95.6). Dreams can arise from the natural operation of the body, or they can be caused by external factors such as heat or cold, or the influence of the stars. They can also be caused by angels, in cases of divine revelation, or demons. He concludes by stressing that dreams that seem to predict the future cannot cause future events to happen, except when people deliberately choose to enact things that they have dreamt about. "But then the cause of the thing enacted," the theologian notes, "is not the dream, but the*

---

10. Ecclesiasticus 34:6.

freedom of the intellect, or rather its instability." Otherwise, if dreams seem to reflect the future, it is only through coincidence.

Lazy Student: Give me an example of this [dreams reflecting the future through coincidence].

Theologian: First I will give you two examples, so you will understand how many people are so deluded by dreams that even when awake they believe that they have truly seen what they only apprehended by their interior sense. For I heard from my teacher that a certain priest of our order entered a certain village, where he found a woman who was so demented that she believed that she was transported through the air during the night with Diana and other women.[11] When the priest tried to get rid of this perfidy with salubrious words, the stubborn woman asserted that she trusted more in her own experience. The priest said to her, "let me be there when you next go out." She responded, "certainly, and you will see me going out, if you please, with proper witnesses present."

Therefore, in order for this zealot of souls[12] to convince the silly woman, when the day came that the old woman had set for her journey the priest was there along with [several] trustworthy men. Then the woman got into a small tub used for making dough, which had been placed on a bench, and sat down. And after applying malefic words and an unguent, she fell asleep with her head lolling backward. And immediately through the operation of a demon she had such a powerful dream about Lady Venus and other superstitious things that in her joy she cried out in a low voice. And by clapping her hands she moved the small tub in which she sat so much that, falling precipitously from the high bench, it bruised the head of the woman lying under it more than a bit.[13] And so the priest rebuked the woman, who had now woken up and was lying motionless on the ground: "Pray tell, where are you? Were you with Diana just now, you who, by the attestation of those

11. The pagan goddess Diana and a group of women believed to travel at night in her train, as described in the early tenth-century canon *Episcopi* (see note 16 below).

12. A favorite term of praise within the Dominican reform movement. See Anne Huijbers, *Zealots for Souls: Dominican Narratives of Self-Understanding During Observant Reforms, c. 1388–1517* (Berlin: De Gruyter, 2018), 228.

13. The implication seems to be that the woman fell out of the tub, then the tub fell on her.

present, never got out of that tub?" By these actions and through these salubrious words, he brought a soul to renounce this error.

Something similar is found in the life of the blessed Germanus of Auxerre,[14] who, seeing a table being prepared in a certain house one evening, learned with astonishment that the food was set out for the good women,[15] who would eat it during the night. Then, keeping watch that same night, he saw a multitude of demons in the form of women sitting at the table, whom he ordered not to depart. He woke the whole family and asked if they recognized the ones eating. When they said that they were their neighbors, he sent them to the houses of each one, and all were found in their beds. The demons were then commanded to reveal themselves, and they disclosed how they deceived these people.

The reason and cause of these things is given in [Case] 26, question 5, [canon] *Episcopi*,[16] where it says, following the Council of Ancyra: Indeed it is Satan, who transforms himself into an angel of light, who, when he has seized the mind of a certain woman and subjugated her to himself through infidelity, immediately transforms himself into the form and likeness of different women, and deluding her mind, which he holds captive, through dreams, he leads her down very devious paths, now showing her joyful things, now sorrowful things, now unknown people.[17] And while the soul alone suffers this, someone lacking in faith will suppose that it happens not in spirit but in the body. You will find many such things in this same place concerning the visions of dreaming people.

14. A bishop in early fifth-century Gaul (ca. 378–448).

15. "Good women" or "good ones" referred to spirits thought to enter houses and to be placatable through offerings of food.

16. C. 26 q. 5 c. 12, as codified in Gratian's *Decretum* (on legal citations of this sort, see note 24 in the chapter above translating Claude Tholosan's *So That the Errors of Magicians and Witches . . .*). During the Middle Ages, the canon *Episcopi* was thought to have been issued by the early fourth-century Council of Ancyra, giving it great antiquity and authority. In fact, the oldest known version comes from an early tenth-century canon law collection by Regino of Prüm. The Latin text can be found (inter alia) in Hansen, *Quellen*, 38–39; English translations in Kors and Peters, *Witchcraft in Europe*, 61–63; Maxwell-Stuart, *Witch Beliefs and Witch Trials*, 47–48.

17. The text of the canon actually reads "now joyful things, now sorrowful things, now people known [to the woman], now unknown."

The chapter ends with the theologian relating an account about a young Dominican who dreamed that he would be elected pope. Despite the fact that nothing about him suggested that he would rise to high office in the church, he hoped the dream might prove true, as indeed it did, in a way. One year during Carnival, when "the younger brothers in the convent sometimes are accustomed to stage playful portrayals of the supreme pontiff and the Roman curia," this young man was chosen to play the role of the pope. This, the theologian explains, is an example of a dream being connected to a future event only through coincidence.

Book 5, Chapter 1: What different colors signify in Holy Scripture. That people's minds are deluded in three ways. And concerning troops and riders in the night, what they signify for good or evil.

Finally, in the fifth book about the qualities of ants, it remains to address witches and their deceptions. Ants are varied in color, as some are black, others red or pale. Different kinds of vices can be understood through these colors, although these animals may be good in themselves, just as all God's creatures. For according to the blessed Gregory,[18] just as the purity and cleanliness of the virtues is normally signified through white and lustrous clothing, so the foulness of the vices is signified through colors deviating to a greater or lesser degree from white, as scripture reports.

This is what the blessed John saw in Revelation 6[:1–8], [where] the color of one of the four horses was black. For the first was described as white, the second red, the third black, and the fourth pale. According to the gloss, the white horse should be understood [as signifying] Christ's purest flesh; the red, those who deceive people by appearing to be religious or virtuous; the black, those who have obvious vices; and the pale horse, like the color of death, those who persecute good people. Those mounted on three such horses[19] represent three kinds

---

18. Gregory the Great (ca. 540–604), an important early medieval religious authority and later pope (r. 590–604).

19. I.e., all but the white one.

of demons that control evil people, because all the ranks of evil people in this life are instructed and directed by certain demons.

The lazy student then asks how "witches and superstitious people" are deceived by demons. The theologian responds that "the human spirit, in the exile of this life, weighed down by the mass of the body and held in its prison, is deceived by illusions in many ways," and that "there are innumerable examples of how people's senses are deluded by demons." The lazy student quickly refines his question to just one kind of vision: "We have sometimes heard from old people that they, so they asserted, saw during the night a host of armed men, as it were, in various guises—of armed men, of horses, of chariots, and the like. I want to know what truth there is in this." The theologian begins with examples of such visions from the Bible (especially the Book of Joshua and 2 Maccabees), from the historian Josephus's Jewish War, *and from Gregory the Great's* Homilies. *He then turns to contemporary examples, including the one below.*

Also, at the time when the electors of the Holy Empire were meeting in a diet in Nuremberg on matters of faith for the good of the kingdom of Bohemia,[20] on a certain day many bishops gathered together in a conclave, along with doctors of both theology and canon law, [to discuss] the same matter. The archbishop of Mainz was there, the bishop of Würzburg, of Augsburg, and, if I remember correctly, of Bamberg. And I was there, of lesser rank and the least among them. When the laity withdrew, after matters of faith had been dealt with, the lord [archbishop] of Mainz, whom I have already mentioned, a very diligent and trustworthy man, related to the aforesaid [group] the following. He named to us a knight from the Rhineland, whom he had known well, whose son was then still alive.[21] This knight had always outshone almost all the nobles of Lower Germany, being altogether fearless in matters of war. Because of his boldness and courage, he

---

20. Nider was prior of the Dominican house in Nuremberg from 1427 until early 1429. The diet referred to here, however, is most likely the one that assembled in March 1432, when Nider was again in Nuremberg as part of a delegation from the Council of Basel seeking to open direct negotiations with the heretical Hussites in Bohemia.

21. Nider never mentions the son again and never clarifies the fate of the knight himself. The implication seems to be that the story took place some years earlier, and since that time the knight had died but his son still lived.

carried out grievous attacks, and sometimes bore them from others, owing to which he was wont to ride out not just during the day but also at night to places where he wanted to go.

One night, therefore, he wanted to ride through a forest near the Rhine together with his servants, and he began to do so. Before they reached the end of the forest, beyond which lay a broad field, he sent a servant ahead, as is the usual practice of those who fear ambushes, so that from the edge of the forest he might see whether any kind of ambush had been set in the field. Such things would be visible under the radiant moon or shining stars. When he reconnoitered through the branches of the trees, as ordered, the servant saw a wondrous troop approaching on horses along the length of the field. He then reported what he had observed to the knight, who said, "let's wait for a little while, because it's likely that others will follow [as] a rearguard for this troop. We will hasten to them, and we will find out whether those who went before are enemies or friends. We will not be [so] apprehensive of [just] a few [men]."

After waiting for some time, the knight left the woods with his men, entered the field, and observed no one except a rider mounted on a horse and leading another horse in hand, following his [companions] at a distance. The knight approached him and asked who he was, with these words: "Aren't you my cook?" For it had seemed to him thus from a distance, but the knight's cook had died just a little while ago. He answered, "I am, lord." "What are you doing here," said the knight, "and who are these who came before you?" The dead man answered him, "lord, these who went before are such-and-such nobles and men-at-arms"—he called many by name—"who must be in Jerusalem this night, and me with them, for this is my punishment." Then the knight [said], "what is the meaning of that horse that you are leading, with no rider?" "It is at your service," he replied, "if you want to come with me to the Holy Land. Rest easy, by Christian faith, departing and returning. I will bring you back alive, if you heed my warnings." Then the knight [said], "I have sought to do astonishing things all my life; this will be another." Although his servants tried to dissuade him, the knight leapt from his horse, mounted the horse of the dead man, and both riders disappeared from the servants' sight.

The following day, while the servants waited as planned, the knight and the dead man returned to the place where they had first met. Then the dead man said to the knight, "lest you believe that this vision was altogether imaginary, keep two rare things that I give to you to remember me by." At which point he offered him a small cloth of salamander[22] and a knife in a scabbard. "When the first becomes dirty," he said, "clean it with fire; it will not harm it. Handle the second carefully, because anyone wounded by it will be poisoned." And then the dead man vanished from the knight's sight.

From these [examples], the wise reader will be able to gather that nocturnal troops are sometimes seen by good people as well as bad ones. Whoever wants to know more about the nature of such things should read the final section of Lord William of Paris's *De universo*,[23] and he will see that I have not deviated from his opinions.

The chapter ends with the lazy student asking if these apparitions are really spirits of the dead, and the theologian responds that this is possible, but also "sometimes these kinds of apparitions are caused, either when one is sleeping or awake, through the agency of good or evil spirits in order to instruct or deceive the living."

Book 5, Chapter 3: What winter and cold signify. Concerning the seven practices of witches, how they eat children, how they openly profess that art, and whether witchcraft may be undone without sin.

Severe cold falling upon ants' eggs hampers their offspring. Either it delays their birth or it kills them outright. For the chill of snow and severity of winter steals away life from the living and often harms that which gives life. The cold can be understood as the hearts of evil people, which are estranged from the heat of charity and the sun of justice but are full of the torpor of malice or faithlessness, about which

22. That is, a substance that cannot burn, named for the lizard that legendarily could not be harmed by fire.
23. William of Auvergne (ca. 1180–1249), a theologian at the University of

Paris and later bishop of Paris, wrote influential works on the nature of demons and spirits.

it is said in the final [chapter] of Proverbs [31:21], concerning a valiant woman: She will not fear for her home in the cold of the snow. Whence the gloss [states]:[24] The hearts of evil people are cold as snow, chilled by the torpor of faithlessness. Concerning which it is said in Matthew 24[:12]: Because iniquity had abounded, the charity of many shall grow cold. [Their] hearts are oppressed by that snow that, falling from the sky in darkness, still presumes owing to pride to declare itself to be like an angel of light. And it displays a snow-white garment, which is proper only for God and his angels, plainly [intending] to signal by this snow-white garment the brightness of its virtue. Moreover, this woman will not fear for her home in the cold of the snow, because she believes in God, who says that the gates of hell shall not prevail against her.[25] For all her servants are clothed with double garments,[26] clearly the wisdom to uncover heresies and the patience to bear the blows of manifest enemies. Or they are clothed with double garments because they have the promise of the life that is now and that is to come. Now they are aided by God, lest they falter, and then [in the afterlife] they will be enriched in blessedness by the divine vision. Also they are clothed in double garments, one being the garment of work, the other of understanding, namely in faith and in deeds, until they are imbued with the sacraments and examples of the Redeemer. All this is in the gloss.

By the cold, therefore, which is quite harmful to the procreation of ants, we can understand witches' superstitions. For a witch is called, as it were, "one who does evil," or "one who keeps evil faith,"[27] both of which are found in witches who injure their neighbors through superstitious works.

Lazy Student: From the blessed Isidore,[28] I know that there are many kinds of superstitions. But because you have made mention of witches, please now tell me in how many ways they can harm their neighbors.

---

24. The *glossa ordinaria*, or ordinary gloss, was the standard commentary on the Bible.

25. The gloss actually reads "against him."

26. Again from Proverbs 31:21.

27. The puns are more effective in Latin: *maleficus enim dicitur quasi male faciens vel male fidem servans.*

28. Isidore of Seville (ca. 560–636), whose *Etymologies* served as an

Theologian: Seven ways occur to me by which they can do harm in regard to things that pertain to human beings, but only if God permits it. Nor do they directly inflict an action or a passion on the people whom they are said to harm, but rather they are said to injure them through words, rites, or deeds, as if through a pact entered with demons. For demons inflict these injuries directly. One way is that they cause a wicked love in some man for some woman, or in some woman for some man. Another is when they manage to engender hatred or envy in someone. A third is [found] in those people who are said to be bewitched, so that they are unable to use their reproductive force on a woman, or conversely females on a man. A fourth is when they cause a person to become sick in some part of their body. A fifth is when they deprive someone of life. A sixth is when they deprive someone of the use of reason. A seventh is when they seek to injure someone in any of the aforesaid ways in their possessions or animals.

Lazy Student: I would like to be informed thoroughly about all these things, because some people either deny them altogether, or ascribe them solely to natural causes, or do not admit to some part of them.

Theologian: It would be of little use to know such things thoroughly. In fact, it might possibly do harm to some. For it would require one to examine prohibited books or other superstitious things that it would be useless to read through when time is so short. Nor is there any need to know such things extensively, certainly not for you, who are not required [to do so] as a condition of your rank. Nevertheless, I will give you some examples and instruction suited to your request, which I have partly from members of our faculty,[29] and partly from the experience of a certain honest and trustworthy secular judge, who through inquiries and confessions and direct experience both public and private learned about many such things, with whom I have often conferred extensively and in depth; namely, Lord Peter, a citizen of Bern in the diocese of Lausanne, who has burned many witches of both sexes and driven others from the territory of the dominion of Bern.[30] I also conferred [about these matters] with Lord Benedict, a monk of the

encyclopedic reference work in medieval Europe.

29. The theological faculty of the University of Vienna.

30. At this time, Bern was a city-state with territory extending high into the Alps (the Bernese Oberland). At least three men named Peter served

order of Saint Benedict. Although he is now a very devout man [living] in Vienna in a reformed monastery, about ten years ago while living in the secular world he was a necromancer, a great jongleur,[31] and a trickster, famous and well known among the secular nobility. Likewise, I heard some of what follows from an inquisitor of Autun, who was a zealous reformer in our order's convent in Lyon, and who interrogated many people accused of witchcraft in the diocese of Lyon.[32]

As this inquisitor and Lord Peter reported to me, and as is generally known, there are or there recently were within the jurisdiction of the dominion of Bern certain witches of both sexes who, against the inclination of human nature, indeed against the nature of all species of animals except only for that of the wolf, devour and are accustomed to eat babies of their own kind. For in the village of Boltigen,[33] in the diocese of Lausanne, a certain powerful witch called Scaedeli was captured by the aforesaid Peter, the judge in that place. He confessed that, in a household in that area where a man and wife lived together, he killed around seven of the woman's babies in the womb through his witchcraft, one after the other, so that for many years she always miscarried. He did likewise to all the breeding animals in this same household, which brought forth no living offspring during these years, as the outcome of this matter showed. When the aforesaid wretch was questioned about whether and how he was guilty of these things, the crime was laid bare. He said that he had placed a lizard beneath the threshold of the door of the house, and if it were removed he predicted that fertility would be restored to the inhabitants. When that serpent was looked for under the threshold, however, it was not found, perhaps because it had been rendered back into dust, [so] they removed the dust or dirt beneath [the threshold], and in that very year fertility was restored to the wife and all the draft animals of the household. He

as bailiffs in the upper Simme valley, where Nider's accounts of witchcraft take place, during the period that he might be describing: Peter von Greyerz (1392–1406), Peter Wendschatz (1407–10), and Peter von Ey (1413–17). See Ostorero et al., *Imaginaire*, 223–31.

31. An itinerant minstrel, juggler, and general entertainer who would have performed magic tricks at noble courts.

32. Autun is about one hundred miles north of Lyon in eastern France. On this man's possible identity, see Mercier and Ostorero, *L'énigme de la Vauderie de Lyon*, 210–21.

33. In the upper Simme valley, roughly twenty miles south of Bern.

[Scaedeli] confessed all this under torture, not voluntarily, and finally he was delivered to the flames by the aforesaid judge.

Then I learned from the aforesaid inquisitor, who reported to me this very year that in the diocese of Lausanne certain witches cooked and ate their own newborn babies. The way in which they learned such an art was, so he said, that the witches came to a certain assembly and, by their action, they saw a demon [appear] visibly in the assumed likeness of a human being. The disciple had to swear to this demon to deny Christianity, never to adore the Eucharist, and to trample on the cross whenever he could do so secretly.

Moreover, it was commonly known, the aforesaid judge Peter told me, that in the territory of Bern, thirteen babies had been devoured by witches within a short period of time, which was why public justice was so harshly inflamed against such killers of their own kin. When Peter had questioned a certain captured witch about how they ate babies, she responded, "this is [our] method. We lie in wait for babies who have not yet been baptized, and also especially for baptized ones if they are not protected with the sign of the cross and prayers. Through our ceremonies, we kill them, lying in their cribs or at their parents' side, and afterward they are thought to have been smothered or killed in another way. Then we take them back out of their coffins secretly and stealthily. We boil them in a cauldron until, with the bones removed, nearly all the flesh is rendered such that it can be slurped up or drunk. Out of this, from the more solid material we make an ointment fit for our desires and arts and transmutations. From the more liquid or fluid matter we refill a bottle or flask. He who drinks from this, with the addition of a few ceremonies, immediately is made an accomplice and master of our sect."

Moreover, another young witch who was captured and burned—although in the end, so I believe, he was truly penitent—revealed this method more clearly. A little while before, he had escaped the grasp of the said judge Peter, along with his wife, a witch who could not be persuaded [to repent]. Captured [again] by the judge in Bernese territory with his wife, and kept apart from her in a separate tower, the young man said, "if I can obtain forgiveness for my enchantments,[34] I would

34. *facinorum.*

willingly disclose everything that I know about witches. For I see that I will have to die."[35] And when he had heard from learned men that he would be able to obtain complete forgiveness if he truly repented, then he happily offered himself to death, and he revealed how he was originally infected. "The manner," he said, "in which I was seduced is this. First, on a Sunday before the holy water is consecrated, the future disciple must enter a church with the masters [of the sect], and there before them deny Christ, his faith, baptism, and the universal church. Then he must give homage to the 'masterling,' that is, the little master.[36] For so they call the demon, and not otherwise. Finally he drinks from the bottle mentioned above. When this is done, he immediately feels that he conceives and holds within himself images of our arts and principal rites. In this way I was seduced, and my wife, who I believe is so stubborn that she would rather suffer the fire than confess the least bit of the truth. But alas, we are both guilty."

Everything was found to be true, just as the young man said. For after having confessed, he was seen to die in [a state of] great contrition. His wife, however, convicted by testimony, would confess nothing of the truth, either under torture or in death. Instead, after the fire had been prepared by the executioner, she cursed him with the worst kind of words, and thus she was burned. It is clear from this how harmful is the cold of faithlessness that kills so many babies and newborns.

Lazy Student: Is it permitted to remove witchcraft from some place?

Theologian: Ancient [authorities] deny this, modern ones allow it, and both are right. But a sole and single distinction must be made. Because either it [witchcraft] can be removed by another act of witchcraft or through the illicit rites of another witch, and that is certain to be illicit—truly, better that a person should die than agree to such things—or it can be removed without new superstitious operations, as through moving something from one place to another, just as has been said about the lizard's dust, and that is allowed. [Here is] an example of the first situation. Now, the inquisitor of Autun told me

---

35. The forgiveness he seeks here is spiritual, not legal.

36. The text itself explains the use of the diminutive form: *magisterulo, id est parvo magistro.*

what means of removing witchcraft or avenging oneself against a witch were practiced in his time. Someone who had been harmed in his person or possessions came to a witch seeking to know the one who had done the harm. The witch then poured liquefied lead repeatedly into water, until, through the operation of a demon, some image would be seen in the lead. When this was seen, the witch asked [her client], "in which part [of his body] do you want your witch to be injured and to recognize him by this injury?"[37] And when [her client] chose a place, the witch immediately made a gouge or wound with a knife in the same part of the image that shone in the lead, and she indicated where the criminal would be found. She did not reveal his name, but experience attests that the witch was found to have been wounded in just the same way as his lead image.

Book 5, Chapter 4: Who necromancers might be, how they sometimes receive a wicked reward from demons, how witchcraft is impeded by divine providence, and how they [witches] rouse storms.

Ants lacking wings or venturing too far from their nests are easily killed by other animals, wherefore those with wings lift themselves up, lest they should become prey for the beasts of the earth. And through wings the virtues are understood, because by such [wings of virtue] good people are carried far. Whence Ezekiel 3[:12–13] says, after describing flying animals: I heard behind me the voice of a great commotion [saying] "blessed be the glory of the Lord from his place," and the voice of the winged animals striking each against the other. The blessed Gregory explains this in book 24 of his *Morals*:[38] For what ought we to perceive by the wings of animals except the virtues of the saints, those who, while they disdain earthly things, are raised up to heaven in flight? Whence it is rightly said by Isaiah [40:31]: Those who trust in the Lord, they shall renew their strength, they shall

---

37. Throughout this passage, the witch performing the counterrite is specified as female (*malefica*), while the witch who initially injured her client is referred to as male (*maleficus*).

38. Gregory the Great (ca. 540–604), *Moralia in Job* 24.8.

take up wings as eagles. The flying animals then strike one another in turn with their wings, because the minds of the saints, insofar as they desire higher things, are roused in turn by their mutual virtues when considering each other. For one strikes me with his wing who, through the example of his own sanctity, incites me to better things. And I strike with my wing a neighboring animal if ever I present to another a good work that he should imitate.

In a moral sense, those ants who are not winged with virtues or who recklessly venture too far out past the boundaries of their home, namely the Catholic church, and so fall into perfidy are easily devoured by bears, which can be understood as witches and necromancers. Likewise this is shown by those simpleminded boys who were devoured by bears when they left their parents' houses and mocked Elisha, as we read in 4 Kings 2 [:23–24].[39]

Lazy Student: Because you mentioned necromancers, I would like to know if there is any difference between them and witches, and if so, what might their activities be?

Theologian: They are properly called necromancers who, through superstitious rites, offer to raise the dead from the earth in order to speak about hidden matters. It was a diviner of this sort who thought she had raised or summoned Samuel at Saul's behest, so that he should reveal to the king the outcome of the war, in 1 Kings 28.[40] The worst of this sort was Simon Magus, who presented his power [as being] above that of the prince of the apostles and feigned raising a dead man.[41] By adapting the usage, however, they are called necromancers who,

39. Some boys mocked the prophet Elisha on the road to the city of Bethel. He cursed them, and they were attacked by two bears that emerged from a nearby forest. 4 Kings in the medieval Vulgate is more commonly designated 2 Kings (1–2 Kings in the Vulgate becoming 1–2 Samuel).

40. I.e., 1 Samuel 28; the account of the famous "witch" of Endor, called here (as she is in the medieval Vulgate) a "pythoness" (*phitonissa*). This term derived from the ancient Pythian oracle at Delphi. The standard medieval interpretation was that the spirit appearing to Saul was not really the dead prophet Samuel but a demon in his form. Hence Nider's statement that she only "thought" she had summoned the prophet.

41. In Acts 8:9–24, Simon was a magician in Samaria who tried to buy the power of the Holy Spirit from the Apostle Peter. In the apocryphal Acts of Peter, Simon engaged in several contests of power with Peter, at one point pretending to revive the dead.

through pacts with demons, predict the future by means of certain rituals, or who discover certain hidden matters through the revelation of demons, or who harm those around them by witchcraft and are themselves often harmed by demons.[42]

There was in Vienna, and still lives there today in the monastery called "Of the Scots,"[43] a brother of the order of Saint Benedict whom I discussed in the previous chapter. While living in the secular world, he was a very famous necromancer, for he had demonic books about necromancy, and in accordance with them he lived quite miserably and dissolutely for a long time. However, he had a sister, a very devout maiden in the order of Penitents, through whose prayers, so I think, her brother was plucked out from the demon's maw. Driven by remorse, he went to various reformed monasteries in various places, seeking to be given the habit of the holy monastic life. But because he was gigantic in stature and terrifying in appearance, and excelled in [both] witchcraft and [magical] entertainments,[44] hardly anyone trusted him. Eventually received into the aforesaid monastery, however, he changed both his name and his life with that entry. For he began to be called Benedict, and, following the Rule of the blessed father Benedict,[45] he made such progress that within a few years he became a model of the religious life. He was appointed to the office of prior and elevated, on account of his popularity, to the pulpit for the laity, becoming a preacher to the people.

While he was still a novice, as I heard from his own report, he endured much distress from the demons whom he had left behind. For when on a certain day he had confessed sacramentally and vomited up the poison of his corrupt life in hope of forgiveness, the following

42. Here it might be better to translate *maleficiis* as "by harmful magic" than "by witchcraft," but Nider's overall point is to blur the distinction between necromancers and witches.

43. The Benedictine abbey of "Our Dear Lady of the Scots," still known as the Schottenstift (Scottish Abbey) in Vienna.

44. Literally, "he was a leader of others in *maleficiis* and *ioculationibus*."

Again here it might be better to translate *maleficiis* as "harmful magic," contrasted with the entertaining magic tricks performed by a *ioculator*, i.e., a jongleur (see note 31 above).

45. Benedict of Nursia (ca. 480–547) wrote the basic governing document subsequently followed by all Benedictine monks.

night, while holding a lamp in his hands, he sensed that a demon was present. And indeed the demon knocked the lamp out of the novice's hands with a violent blow, and it tried to do him quite serious harm. But the soldier of Christ conquered the tyranny of this bear, because he had already taken up the wings of virtue, by which, through holy prayers, he was freed from the beast's mouth.

Moreover, I likewise heard from the judge Peter, mentioned above,[46] that in the territory of Bern and in places adjacent to it witchcraft, as described above, had been practiced by many people for around sixty years. The first originator of these practices was a certain man called Scavius, who dared to boast publicly about this, [saying] that whenever he wanted, he could make himself [seem] like a mouse in the eyes of all his rivals and slip out of the hands of his mortal enemies. And in this way, so it is said, he often escaped the deadly clutches of his enemies. But when divine justice wanted to put an end to his wickedness, his enemies at last warily spied him sitting in a bathhouse. In that place, when he did not suspect that anyone was setting a trap for him, he was unexpectedly pierced through the window by swords and spears and died there pitifully for his crimes.

Nevertheless, he passed on the knowledge of his deceits to a disciple who was called Hoppo, and who made the aforementioned Scaedeli a master of witchcraft.[47] These two knew how to carry off a third part of the dung, hay, grain, or whatever else from a neighbor's field to their own field whenever they wanted, without anyone seeing; how to cause truly enormous hailstorms and destructive winds with lightning; how to fling children walking next to water in full view of their parents into that water, [but] with no one seeing them; how to cause sterility in people and draft animals; how to harm those around them in their possessions and their persons; how to drive horses mad beneath their riders, if they grasped the stirrup while mounting; how to travel from place to place, so they think, through the air; how to emit a terrible stench whenever they might be captured; how to incite great trembling in the hands and minds of those seeking to capture them; how to reveal things hidden to others and predict some future events; how to see things that are not there as if they were really

46. Peter of Bern. See note 30 above.   47. On Scaedeli, see *Anthill* 5.3.

present; how to kill whomever they want by a lightning strike; and how to cause other destructive things, where and when God's justice permitted these things to be done.

Lazy Student: I would like to know two things here. First, whether demons and their disciples can [really] perform such witchcraft by means of lightning, hailstorms, and the like, of which you spoke, [but] which some doubt. Second, I would like to know whether such wretches admit that divine works might impede them in their machinations.

Theologian: To the first, I respond that beyond doubt they can [do these things], but not unless God allows it. For in Job 1 and 2, the demon, after he had received power from God, immediately brought it about that the Sabeans bore away five hundred teams of oxen and five hundred donkeys; then that fire falling from heaven burned up seven thousand sheep; that three troops of Chaldeans carried off three thousand camels; that seven sons and three daughters perished from a furious wind blowing through the house, along with many servants, [although] always with one spared; and that the holy man's body was struck with a terrible ulcer, and his wife and three of his friends troubled him grievously.[48] Whence the holy doctor says:[49] It is necessary to confess that with God's permission demons can cause a disturbance in the air, rouse the winds, and make fire fall from the sky. For although corporeal nature does not obey the command of either good or evil angels in terms of taking on forms, but only that of God the Creator, nevertheless corporeal nature was made to obey spiritual nature in terms of local movement. Evidence of this is found in human beings. For the limbs are moved at the command of the will alone, so that they pursue the task disposed by the will. Therefore, whatever can be done by local movement alone can be done through the natural power of not only good but also evil angels, unless prohibited by divine power. Moreover, winds and rain and other aerial disturbances of this sort can be caused solely by the movement of vapors released from the earth or water. Thus the natural power of a demon suffices to cause such things. This from Thomas. For God is

48. These afflictions are described in Job 1:14–19 and 2:7–11.

49. Thomas Aquinas (1225–1274) was a leading Dominican theologian;

here from his *Expositio super Iob ad litteram* 1.3.

accustomed to inflict rightly through demons, as through his execu-
tioners, the evils that are produced in the world, exacted for our sins.
About this the gloss on Psalm 104[:16],[50] "He called a famine upon
the land and he destroyed every staff of bread," says thus: God sends
these evils through evil angels who have been put in charge of such
things. "He calls a famine" therefore means [that he calls] the angel
in charge of famine. This from the gloss.

Further, to the second doubt, you will undoubtedly have learned
that witches can be impeded in many ways. For many have confessed
this under torture, some grudgingly, but others willingly. And to summarize what I gathered from talking with the aforesaid Peter, there are
five ways through which they are greatly impeded, sometimes completely, sometimes partly, sometimes so that they cannot act against a
person directly, sometimes so that they cannot act against someone's
friends; namely, by maintaining sound faith or keeping God's commandments out of love for God, by protecting oneself with the sign
of the cross and prayer, by honoring the rites and ceremonies of the
church, by properly exercising public justice, and by ruminating on
Christ's passion in word and thought. Concerning the first and second,
Peter told me such examples as he had heard from the witches mentioned above. "When," he said,[51] "some simple but dishonest person
called on me, as a witch, to end the life of his enemy, or to cause him
grievous bodily harm by a lightning bolt or some other means, I called
the masterling,[52] that is, the demon, who replied to me that he could
do neither. 'Does he have sound faith,' he said, 'and does he protect
himself with the sign of the cross? On account of that, I cannot harm
his person, but I can harm him, if you would like, in one eleventh part
of his produce in the field.'"

I knew a certain elderly maiden in the lands of the diocese of
Constance, who was named Earnestine.[53] She was [like] a mother and a
model to all the maidens living in the vicinity, and she had the greatest
confidence in the sign of the life-giving cross and the passion of Christ.

---

50. 105:16 in the Hebrew
numbering.

51. Having mentioned multiple
examples, Nider then presents only a
single (male) witch's account.

52. See note 36 above.

53. *Seriosa.*

She also remained of her own will in a cottage in a poor village in an area where witches were sometimes found to reside. A friend of hers had been seriously injured in his foot through witchcraft, which could not be healed through any art. After many remedies had been applied in vain, the aforesaid maiden visited the sick man, who asked her to apply some blessing to his foot. She nodded and silently said only the Lord's Prayer and Apostles' Creed while twice making the sign of the life-giving cross. The sick man then immediately felt himself to be healed, and he wanted to know, as a remedy for future [afflictions], what enchantment the maiden has used. She replied, "through wicked or weak faith, you do not adhere to the divine and approved practices of the church, and you repeatedly apply prohibited remedies to your infirmities. For that reason you suffer harm, sometimes in your body but always in your soul. But if you would put your trust in the power of permissible prayers and signs, you would often be cured quite easily. For I used nothing on you except the Lord's Prayer and the Apostles' Creed, and now you are healed."

Moreover, it is certain that witches confess that their witchcraft is impeded by observing and honoring the rites of the church, such as sprinkling blessed water, taking consecrated salt, the permissible use of consecrated candles on Candlemas and palms on Palm Sunday, and the like, because the church performs exorcisms by means of such things in order to diminish the powers of demons.

Concerning public justice, all the witches mentioned above have testified by word and experience that when they are arrested by officials of public justice, all their power as witches is weakened. Thus when the oft-mentioned judge Peter wanted his deputies to arrest the aforesaid Scaedeli, such trembling struck their hands and bodies and such a foul stench filled their nostrils that they almost despaired of venturing to lay hold of the witch. The judge said to them, "lay hold of the wretch without fear, because when he is touched by public justice, he will lose all the powers of his wickedness." And so it proved to be.

Concerning the fifth [means of impeding witchcraft], the judge gave this example. "When," he said, "I had arrested Scaedeli, who was reputed to have done very grave harm in the region by means of hailstorms and to have devastated it with lightning, I asked about the truth of these matters. After the ropes were drawn for the fourth time,[54] he finally gave me this response: 'I cause hailstorms easily, yet I cannot do harm as I please, but only against those who have forsaken God's help. Truly, those who protect themselves with the sign of the cross will not die from my lightning.'" The judge [then asked] him, "how do you go about raising storms and hail?" The criminal replied, "first, in a field, we beseech the chief of all demons with certain words that he should send one of his [servants] to strike the person designated by us. Then, when a demon has come, we sacrifice a black hen at some crossroads by throwing it high into the air. After the demon seizes this, it obeys [us] and immediately rouses the air by casting down hail and lightning, not always in the place we intended but according to the permission of the living God." The judge continued with a third question: "Cannot such storms roused by you and by demons be alleviated in some way?" [Scaedeli] answered, "they can be through these [words]: I conjure you, hail and winds, by the five divine nails of Christ,[55] which pierced Christ's hands and feet, and by the four evangelists, Saints Matthew, Mark, Luke, and John, that you should come down melted into water."

From this it is now clear that the mercy and wisdom of almighty God, which reaches mightily from one end [of the earth] to the other,[56] sweetly disposes the witchcraft of awful people and demons, so that, while they seek to diminish Christ's kingdom and to weaken faith through their faithlessness, they instead strengthen these and implant them more strongly in the hearts of many. Indeed, many benefits for the faithful can come out of the aforesaid evils, because through them faith is strengthened, the malice of demons is perceived, the mercy and power of God is made manifest, people are moved to act for their own protection, and they are stirred to revere Christ's passion and the rites of the church.

54. An application of torture.

55. While Christ had five wounds (hands, feet, and a spear wound to his side) on the cross, he was generally thought to have been pierced by only three nails (one in each hand and one through both feet). Several versions of the *Anthill* refer to three nails here.

56. Wisdom 8:1.

Book 5, Chapter 7: What feeds slander. How witches sometimes injure judges, how they perceive what is absent, and how they sometimes say contradictory things.

Ants eaten by human beings are harmful to them, but not to all beasts. Indeed, they are beneficial to some, such as bears, for example, which eagerly seek them out. The just are designated by the name of ants, as we saw in previous chapters. To eat, however, is to diminish another life, either in reputation or in sound doctrine. He warned his son about such consumption, who said in Proverbs 23[:20–21]:[57] Do not be in the banquets of drinkers, nor in the revels of those who bring meat to eat, because those devoting themselves to drinking and contributing to a feast—the gloss [adds here] "of slander"—are themselves consumed. The gloss further says there: To bring meat to eat is to state again the faults of those around one during a general derogatory discourse. It continues concerning the punishment for this: Because those who devote themselves to such things are themselves consumed. In contrast to this, it is fitting to give heed to good words containing divine wisdom, by which the soul can legitimately be satisfied. Concerning which Solomon adds in Proverbs 24[:13–14]: Eat honey, my son—the gloss [adds here] "the instruction of wisdom"—because it is good and the honeycomb is very sweet in the throat. So too is the instruction of wisdom to your soul, for when you have found it you will have hope in the last [days], and your hope will not perish. The gloss says: The instruction of wisdom is compared to honey and the honeycomb because, just as they are superior to other food, so it is superior to other teachings.

And also, concerning those who devour human flesh through the vice of slander and through the witchcraft of superstition, it says in Psalms [56:5]:[58] The sons of men whose teeth are weapons and arrows, and their tongues a sharp sword. And Proverbs 30[:14] says about the last of four perverse generations: A generation that has swords for teeth and chews with its molar teeth so that it consumes the needy

---

57. The Book of Proverbs was traditionally ascribed to Solomon, as Nider indicates below.

58. Vulgate Psalm 56:5 varies slightly from Masoretic (Hebrew numbering) Psalm 57:4.

from the earth and the poor from among mankind. Where the gloss [states]: "A generation that has swords for teeth," that is, one that tries to spread its deceits to others, and just as bodies [are killed] by swords, so it kills the souls of those listening by the poison of speech. Whence it is said "so that it consumes," that is, devours, "the needy," that is, the innocent, "and the poor," that is, the humble.

Moreover, it is not good for humans to devour ants, but it is for beasts, such as the bear, because the business of witches and the business of slander delights not the just but the deceitful. A symbol of which [is found] in Daniel 7[:5]: The second beast that arose from the sea was like a bear that stood up on one side, and there were rows of teeth in its mouth and among its teeth, and they said, "arise, devour much flesh."[59] Through this is intimated the threefold harm done by witches, namely [harming] of worldly goods, of human bodies, and of rational minds, which are often injured by witches' practices. Whence Proverbs 17[:11–12]: An evil person always seeks quarrels, but a cruel angel will be sent against him. It is better to meet a bear whose cubs have been stolen away than a fool trusting in his own folly. Whence the gloss [adds]: The cruel angel is an unclean spirit that is sent from God against sinners, that he should afflict them in the present as [he once did] the Egyptians. Through evil angels he sent against them the anger of his displeasure. And it continues: The bear can be understood as the malice of the ancient enemy, whose offspring we steal away when we add those who were his sons to the sons of God by catechizing and baptizing them. And this is often more easily done than to recall a heretic to proper faith or to lead a Catholic behaving wrongly back to good works.

Lazy Student: You say that witches and those who are false in faith can be understood in terms of beasts devouring ants. Give an

---

59. Nider deviates somewhat from the standard Vulgate text here, which reads: "And behold, another beast like a bear stood up on one side, and three rows were in its mouth and among its teeth, and thus they said to it 'Arise, devour much flesh.'" What the Vulgate renders as rows (*ordines*) were ribs in the Hebrew original and Greek Septuagint, sometimes understood as tusks or fangs, so "rows of teeth" (*ordines dentium*) makes some sense, although it produces the awkward "rows of teeth . . . among its teeth."

example of how they carry out that work by assailing human bodies from health into infirmity.

Theologian: I heard that such beasts would have done wicked things to Judge Peter,[60] whom I discussed previously, for they long strove to avenge themselves on him. But because he had good faith and was accustomed to protect himself diligently with the sign of the cross, being well advised, he generally avoided giving them the opportunity to perform witchcraft [on him]. On account of such prudence, therefore, he avoided harm, except one time when, through his own fault, he did not deserve to be entirely protected by the Lord, as he told me.

He had been accustomed to reside at the castle of Blankenburg in the territory of Bern when he governed that region.[61] After he resigned that office, however, he returned to the city of Bern, where he had a house. Going back one day to the aforesaid castle, where his relative had replaced him in office, Peter wanted to carry out some business there with people he knew. Then a witch and four men who were her companions in wickedness gathered in one place at a late hour, mulling over the devices of their art as best they could, so that they might harm Peter seriously by witchcraft,[62] or kill him, from whom these deceitful schemes lay hidden.

Then, when night came, Peter went to bed, blessing himself with the sign of the cross. But he determined to get up in the night to write some necessary letters, so that he would be able to leave that place early in the morning. Waking, therefore, in the dark of night, it seemed to him that day had come, deceived [as he was] by a false light. He was angry at himself over this, because he thought that he had let the night slip away. Not protecting himself in the usual way, as he ought to have done, he put on his clothes, descended some high stairs to the place where he kept his writing tablets, and found the place locked. Burning with even greater anger at this, he climbed back up toward his bed by

60. Once again, Peter of Bern; see note 30 above.

61. Blankenburg is in the upper Simme valley about five miles from the village of Boltigen; see note 33 above.

62. Here *veneficiis* rather than *maleficiis*.

63. Presumable Peter cursed in German, and Nider renders here what he would have said if he had cursed in Latin.

the stairs that he had [just] descended, grumbling and uttering out of indignation a single, very short curse, as if he would have said "in the name of the devil."[63] And here immediately, [engulfed] in the thickest shadows, Peter was thrown headlong so violently down the aforesaid steps that a servant who slept in a room beneath the stairs was roused and wanted to see what had happened. By the light of the rising sun, he found Peter lying insensible on the ground and bruised all over, bleeding profusely. The whole household was roused, but there was no one who could uncover the cause of the fall. At last, however, with divine grace smiling [on him], Peter regained his senses, although he scarcely recovered his physical health for three weeks. And although he suspected the witches whom he longed to wipe clean from the region, insofar as he could, he did not know the [specific] culprits guilty of this crime carried out against him.

But because there is nothing hidden that is not eventually revealed, it later happened that a certain witch, who was in hiding, went from the region of Bern, where he lived, to the city of Fribourg, in the diocese of Lausanne. One day he sat with others drinking in a tavern and spoke to his companions. "Look," he said, "I see that such a one," whom he named, "is pulling up and stealing the hook that I put in the water near my lodgings to catch fish." They were, however, six long German miles distant from the place,[64] across which he observed the theft through the operation of a demon. Faithful people weighed these words, indicted the criminal, and he was later transferred to prison by judicial order. Harshly interrogated there for two days, he was utterly unwilling to confess anything about his own crimes. On the third day, however, which was a Saturday, when generally out of reverence for the most blessed Virgin a divine service is celebrated in her honor, he was tortured again and vomited up all his poison. For he said that the truth about his previous statements and the theft was borne out by experience, and he confessed that four male witches along with a female witch, whom he named, had thrown Peter headlong [down the

---

64. The German mile was only standardized in the nineteenth century, in relation to the metric system, at 7.5 kilometers, or slightly over 4.5 English miles. Earlier, however, German miles varied widely from region to region. Fribourg is about twenty (English) miles from Bern.

stairs], by that old woman's hand.[65] He also asserted that such wrath arose in the old woman because the judge had not always administered justice to her liking. And he added that on the other two days he was restrained by the devices of demons from being able to confess under torture. But because, so he said, the feast of the blessed Virgin was celebrated with a divine service, he was now free to tell the truth. And so, following the municipal laws of the land, he was finally sent to the fire.

It must be noted, however, that such false prophets, deceived by the Father of Lies, are accustomed sometimes to say entirely contradictory things, as the same Peter reported that he had experienced. For a certain witch was arrested by him and locked in a tower. She, however, had a husband, who was not a master of such witchcraft. Led by curiosity, he hastened to some old woman in that area, whom everyone declared knew the future. When he had come to her as a suppliant, he asked her to tell him if he ought to have any hope that his wife, who had been arrested, might escape from the judge with her life. The old woman answered him, "fear not, she will certainly be freed, nor will she die in captivity." After that, the man became happier, and he met Judge Peter the next day. Peter asked him, "where have you been?" And he said, "I was at the house of a prophetess, who told me that my wife would be freed from your bonds and would not die in captivity." After returning to his lodgings, Peter was called by the captured witch, who said to Peter, "I saw that my husband approached an old woman who foretold that I would be freed. I know that she lies, because tomorrow I will be burned, in accordance with your judgment." When the judge later told this to the husband, who derided him, they waited to see which of the two witches had spoken the truth. But thereafter, on the next day, the burning of the imprisoned woman, carried out through public justice, made clear that the witch who was married to the man had told the truth.

And yet you should not believe, as it appears in the first example, that Peter was literally thrown down the stairs at the hands of witches, who were not physically in the castle. Rather, demons drawn by the

---

65. The Latin stresses the four male witches (*quator viri malefici*) in contrast to one female witch (*malefica*), but also that the woman wielded the operative power here.

witches' sacrifices and ceremonies were there, and they caused Peter's precipitous fall. And in order to deceive the witches' minds, they made it appear in these superstitious people's imagination as if they were there. So too in the second and third examples, something absent was made to appear as present by the impression of a demon on the witches' imagination, just as you heard previously in chapter 1 of the present book, in the words of the holy doctor,[66] and also in chapter 5.

Book 5, Chapter 8: How much sexual pleasure must be shunned. Concerning women dressed as men declaring publicly that they have been sent by God. And concerning three things that rarely hold to the middle; namely, a tongue, a churchman, and a woman, which excel in goodness, but are sometimes the very worst in wickedness.

The carcasses of dead animals are sometimes food for ants. In moral understanding, to eat dead animals is to engage in perverse lust. Hence those who are sometimes seduced by sinful women owing to their hunger for lustful pleasure have eaten dead animals, enjoying God's displeasure in these acts more than a little, as is touched on briefly in Psalm 105[:28],[67] by way of the Israelites: They were, it says, consecrated to Belphegor and ate sacrifices of the dead. Concerning which it is stated more clearly in Numbers 25[:1–4]: The people fornicated with the daughters of Moab, who called them to their sacrifices. And they ate and worshiped their gods. And Israel was consecrated to Belphegor, and God was angered and said to Moses, "take all the leaders of the people and hang them from gibbets under the sun, so that my fury may be turned away from Israel." Israel did all this having been seduced by the hidden machination of the witch Balaam,[68] who through his counsel was the source of this deadly fornication in Israel. About which the gloss [states]: Whoever is a slave to pleasure holds to the teaching of Balaam.

---

66. Thomas Aquinas.

67. 106:28 in the Hebrew numbering.

68. Balaam was a soothsayer, here described as a *maleficus*, serving the Moabites.

How execrable, therefore, is physical fornication, which defiles the temple of God and takes the limbs of Christ and makes them limbs of a prostitute.[69] But even more execrable is fornication in a general sense, which encompasses every kind of sin equally, when the soul, received into fellowship with the word of God and united with it by marriage, is corrupted by the adversary of the one who betrothed himself to it in faith. For the word of God—that is, Christ—is the groom and husband of the pure soul. I have betrothed you all to one husband, said the Apostle, to present a chaste virgin to Christ.[70] Where, therefore, the soul cleaves to its husband and embraces him and hears his word, it receives from him the seed of the word and conceives and has sons—modesty, justice, patience, and all the virtues—so that it may be saved by bearing sons, if it perseveres in faith and charity.[71] If, however, it prostitutes itself with the devil or demons, it will have sons of adultery, namely, sins of every kind. And the gloss of Origen on this passage [Numbers 25] adds:[72] All the sins that we commit, especially if we sin not in some surreptitious way but eagerly, consecrate us to that demon whose task it is to make us commit them. And perhaps we are consecrated to as many demons as sins that we commit, and for that we take up the service of that idol.

Moreover, the bodies of fornicators are deservedly compared to the bodies of fetid animals. Because as Ecclesiasticus 9[:10] says: Every woman who has fornicated shall be trodden upon as dung in the street. Therefore the prophet, after he spoke of those who are mighty drinkers of wine,[73] in which there is lust, adds a little later in Isaiah 5[:25]: Their carcasses became dung in the middle of the streets. For all this, his fury is not turned away, but his hand—that is, the hand of God—is stretched forth.

Lazy Student: In your judgment, are there in our time some good men who are deceived by female magicians or witches?[74]

---

69. 1 Corinthians 6:15.
70. 2 Corinthians 11:2.
71. 1 Timothy 2:15.
72. Origen of Alexandria (ca. 184–253) was an early church father.

The reference here is to his *In Numeros homiliae* 20.3.4.
73. Isaiah 5:22.
74. *per magas vel maleficas.*

Theologian: I suspend my own judgment in the following, but I will report what official word and rumor imparts. We have today a distinguished professor of sacred theology, Brother Henry Kalteisen, an inquisitor of heretical depravity.[75] When last year he became inquisitor in the city of Cologne, as he related to me, he observed that there was a certain maiden near Cologne who went around all the time in men's clothing. She bore weapons and wore dissolute clothes, like one in the paid service of nobles.[76] She danced with men, and drank and feasted so much that she appeared to exceed entirely the proper boundaries of the feminine sex, which she did not deny. And because at that time, just as, alas, today, two men were causing great trouble contending for the episcopal see of Trier,[77] she bragged that she could enthrone one party, just as the maiden Joan, of whom we will speak presently, had done shortly before for King Charles of France, confirming him in his kingship.[78] Indeed, she claimed that she was this same Joan, inspired by God.

When therefore she entered Cologne one day with the young count of Virneburg,[79] who protected and supported her, and before the eyes of the nobility there performed wonders that seemed to be done by magic art, she was carefully investigated and publicly summoned by the aforesaid inquisitor, in order to be examined. It was said that she ripped up a napkin and immediately restored it in the sight of all, and she instantaneously repaired a glass that she had thrown against a wall and shattered, and she demonstrated many similar empty tricks. But this miserable woman refused to obey the orders of the church. The aforementioned count protected her, lest she be captured. Secretly taken by him out of Cologne, she escaped the inquisitor's grasp but not the chains of excommunication. When these were tightened, she left Germany and entered France, where she married a soldier, so that she would not be troubled by ecclesiastical interdict and authority.

75. Kalteisen (ca. 1390–1464), a Dominican theologian, was an inquisitor in the Rhineland and Low Countries early in his career.

76. I.e., a mercenary.

77. The Trier archepiscopal election had been contested in 1430, and the dispute lasted for several years.

78. Joan of Arc (ca. 1412–1431).

79. Virneburg lies about midway between Cologne and Trier.

Thereafter a certain priest, or better yet he should be called a pimp, charmed this magician with amorous words. She finally went back [to Germany] with him and entered the city of Metz,[80] where, living with him as a concubine, she showed clearly to everyone what kind of spirit guided her.

Moreover, there was recently, less than ten years ago, a certain woman in France whom I have already mentioned, a maiden named Joan, famous for her prophetic spirit and miraculous power, so it was thought. She always wore men's clothing, nor could she be softened by any exhortations by doctors of any sort[81] that she should set aside such clothes and remain satisfied with women's clothing, especially since she professed openly that she was a maiden and a woman. "In this masculine dress," she said, "as a sign of future victory, which I proclaim by word and dress, I have been sent by God to help Charles, the true king of France, and to confirm him in his kingship, from which the king of England and duke of Burgundy strive to exile him." For at that time they had joined together in arms and carnage and were grievously oppressing France. Therefore Joan, together with her lord, rode constantly like a soldier, predicted many future successes, participated in some military victories, and accomplished other such wonders that astonished not only France but all Christian kingdoms.[82]

Joan finally became so presumptuous that, having not yet achieved France,[83] she struck out through threatening letters at Bohemia, where there was then a multitude of heretics.[84] Hence both secular and regular clergy and monks were uncertain as to what spirit guided her, diabolical or divine. Some very learned men wrote treatises about this, in which they judged the maiden not only in different but indeed in opposing ways. A few years ago, however, after she had helped King

---

80. Now in northeastern France but at this time in the German empire.

81. Presumably doctors of theology and canon law.

82. During the latter phases of the Hundred Years War (1337–1453), the English and their Burgundian allies controlled most of northern France. Joan convinced Charles VII (r. 1422–61) to have himself formally crowned king

in 1429 (he had hesitated because of a treaty his father, Charles VI, had been forced to sign with the English). She then led French troops in several major battles, including her famous victory at Orléans in early May 1429.

83. I.e., having not yet liberated France completely.

84. Joan dictated a letter to the heretical Hussites on March 23, 1430.

Charles in many ways and established him in his kingdom, by the will of God, so it is believed, she was captured and imprisoned by the English army.[85] A great number of masters of both divine and human law[86] were sent and called for, who examined her for many days. And as I heard from Master Nicolas Amici, licensed in theology, who was the ambassador of the University of Paris,[87] she eventually admitted that she had an angel of God as a familiar spirit, which in the judgment of these very learned men was determined through many conjectures and proofs to be a malign spirit. Since this spirit had turned her into a magician, they surrendered her to be consumed by the flames though public justice, and the king of England gave a detailed written account of these events to our emperor Sigismund.[88]

At the same time, two women appeared in Paris, saying publicly that they had been sent by God in order to help the maiden Joan. And I heard directly from the aforesaid Master Nicolas how they were arrested by the inquisitor of France as magicians or witches, and, after they were examined by many doctors of sacred theology, it was eventually discovered that they were deceived by the ravings of a malign spirit. When one of these women perceived that she had been seduced by an angel of Satan, thanks to these masters' explanation, she repented her undertakings and immediately recanted her error, as she should. The other one, however, remained obstinate and was consumed by the flames.

Lazy Student: I cannot wonder enough how the fragile sex dares to rush into such audacities.

Theologian: Among simple folk like you such things are astonishing, but in the eyes of wise men they are not rare. For there are three things that, by nature, if they exceed the boundaries of their status either by deficiency or by excess, achieve the apex of either goodness or wickedness; namely, a tongue, a churchman, and a woman. If they

85. Joan was actually captured by Burgundian forces on May 23, 1430, and was later transferred to English custody.

86. I.e., canon and civil law.

87. Nicolas Lami (Amici) was the university's ambassador to the Council of Basel.

88. Sigismund I (r. 1433–37). After executing Joan, the English wrote to many of the crowned heads of Europe to justify their action.

are governed by a good spirit, they tend to become extremely good, but if by an evil spirit, then they tend to become extremely bad.

For many kingdoms have been subjugated to the Christian faith by the good ministry of a single tongue—let us illustrate the case of the tongue first—as is clear regarding Christ's apostles and wise preachers. Likewise the tongue of a prudent man can sometimes prevent the ruin of innumerable people. Solomon speaks of this in Proverbs 10[:13, 20–21]: Wisdom is found on the lips of the wise, and a rod to the back of one who lacks judgment. The tongue of the just [is like] choice silver, [but] the heart of the impious [is worth] nothing. The lips of the just teach many; those who are ignorant, however, will die in want of understanding. The cause of this is given in the same book, [Proverbs] 16[:1], because: It is for a person to prepare the soul, and for the Lord to govern the tongue.

Concerning the malice of the tongue, it is said in Ecclesiasticus 28[:13, 16–17]: A testifying tongue brings death. A third tongue stirred up many and scattered them from nation to nation. It has destroyed the fortified cities of the rich and ransacked the houses of the great. Behold, there are many evils. And likewise James 3[:5–8] [describes] what evils the tongue causes. The "third tongue" belongs to those who heedlessly or maliciously interject something between two opposing parties.

We have many examples concerning churchmen. And by churchmen we mean clerics and religious of both sexes. The blessed Jerome speaks about wicked clerics in his letter to Nepotian:[89] A cleric who engages in trade, [going] from poverty to wealth, from obscurity to fame, flee as if [from] the plague. And the blessed Bernard in Sermon 33[:15] on the Song,[90] speaking of clergy, says: If a heretic would rise up openly, he would be cast out and he would wither. If a violent enemy, they would perhaps hide themselves from him—meaning good pastors. But now, whom will they drive out or from whom will they hide themselves?[91] All are friends and all are enemies, all are members of

---

89. Jerome (ca. 347–420) was an early church father; he wrote to Nepotian in 394 about the duties of Christian clergy.

90. Bernard of Clairvaux (1090–1153) was a Cistercian abbot; his sermons on the biblical Song of Songs were among his most famous works.

91. Bernard's original text describes the church, as a singular entity, responding to heretics and enemies.

the same household and none are peaceable, all are neighbors but all seek what is theirs alone. Here the blessed Gregory says in his *Pastoral Care*: No one harms the church more than one who, while acting perversely, has the name and rank of sanctity. For no one presumes to refute him when he transgresses, and the fault spreads forcefully as a model [for others] when the sinner is honored out of reverence for his rank.[92] Concerning religious clergy the blessed Augustine says to Vincentius the Donatist: I plainly confess to your charity, before the Lord our God, who, since I began to serve God, is a witness upon my soul, that as rarely as I have found people better than those who succeed in monasteries, even so I have not found people worse than those who fail in monasteries.[93]

Concerning the malice of women, Ecclesiasticus 25[:22–23] says: There is no head worse than the head of a serpent, and there is no anger above the anger of a woman. It would be more pleasing to abide with a lion or a dragon than to live with a wicked woman. And, among many things about a wicked woman before and after that, it concludes [25:26]: All malice is brief compared to the malice of a woman. Hence Chrysostom on Matthew 19[:10], "It is not expedient to marry": What else is a woman than an enemy of friendship, an inescapable punishment, a necessary evil, a natural temptation, a desirable disaster, a domestic danger, a delightful detriment, an evil nature painted with a good color? Therefore if to send her away is a sin, but to keep her is almost a torture, we must either commit adultery by sending her away or have daily conflicts by keeping her.[94] Finally, Tullius in the second [book] of his *Rhetoric*: Individual desires drive men to each evil deed; a single desire leads women to all evil deeds. For the foundation of

Nider clarifies that he is describing "good pastors."

92. Gregory the Great (ca. 540–604), *Regula pastoralis* 1.2.

93. Augustine of Hippo (354–430), an early church father, from a letter written in 404 (Letter 78), not to Vincentius but to the entire church of Hippo. Donatists were a group of Christians in North Africa who argued that clergy needed to be morally faultless in order to perform their office. Augustine considered Donatists to be heretics.

94. John Chrysostom (ca. 349–407) was an early church father; this passage is from a work that was incorrectly attributed to him during the Middle Ages, the *Incomplete Work on Matthew* (*Opus imperfectum in Matthaeum*) 38.

all the feminine faults lies in nature.[95] And Seneca in his *Proverbs*: A woman either loves or hates, there is no third. For a woman to cry is a lie. There are two kinds of tears in the eyes of women, one of true sorrow and one of artifice. When a woman thinks alone, she thinks of evil things.[96]

Concerning good women, however, there is such praise that one can likewise read about how they have blessed men and also redeemed [entire] peoples, lands, and cities; [women] such as Deborah, Judith, and Esther.[97] Hence the Apostle in 1 Corinthians 7[:13]: If any woman has an unbelieving husband, and he consents to live with her, she should not send the man away. For the unbelieving man is sanctified by the faithful woman. Therefore in Ecclesiasticus 26[:1]: The husband of a good woman is blessed, for the number of his years is double. It says many very praiseworthy things there throughout the entire chapter about the excellence of good women. So does Solomon, or rather the Holy Spirit, throughout the whole last chapter of Proverbs [31], about a valiant woman. The aforesaid [virtues] also shine forth amply in women of the New Testament, primarily in virgins and other holy women who drew faithless peoples to Christianity, such as Magdalene, Catherine, Margaret, Martha, and those like them.[98]

95. Marcus Tullius Cicero (106–43 BCE), a famous Roman orator; again the passage is from a work that was incorrectly attributed to him, *Rhetoric for Herennius* (*Rhetoricum ad Herennium*) 4.23. What I translate here as "evil deed/s" was actually *maleficium/a* in the original text. Cicero clearly meant the term in its earliest and most general sense of a wicked action or crime. Nider, however, undoubtedly also meant to invoke its more specific connotations of witchcraft.

96. Seneca the Younger (ca. 4 BCE–65 CE) was a Roman philosopher and dramatist; yet again these passages are from a work wrongly attributed to him, the *Sayings* (*Sententiae*) of Publilius Syrus (fl. 85–43 BCE).

97. In the biblical Book of Judges, Deborah helped liberate the Israelites from oppression by Jabin, the king of Canaan. In the Book of Judith, Judith ingratiated herself to the Assyrian general Holofernes, only to decapitate him while he was drunk one night. In the Book of Esther, Esther married the Persian king Ahasuerus and protected Jews in Persia from oppression by the grand vizier Haman.

98. Mary Magdalene and Martha of Bethany both appear in the New Testament among the followers of Jesus. No women named Catherine or Margaret appear in the New Testament, but Margaret of Antioch and Catherine of Alexandria were early fourth-century martyrs. Both were also among the saints whom Joan of Arc claimed spoke to her.

So too the whole kingdom of Hungary, long given over to idolatry, was joined to the Catholic faith by Gisele, Christian sister of the emperor, through the king of Hungary, to whom the aforesaid Gisele was given in marriage. Through her the king was converted and [re]named Stephen in baptism, and later, renowned for his miracles, he was canonized, as Vincent sets down in his *Mirror of History*, book 26, chapter 9.[99] Thus also through the Christian maiden Clotilde, born into the line of Burgundy, Clovis, the king of the Franks, was eventually persuaded to abandon idolatry and come to the faith of Christ, along with his kingdom, as Vincent relates in book 22, chapters 4, 5, and 6.[100]

99. Correctly book 15 of *Speculum historiale*. Vincent of Beauvais (ca. 1190–ca. 1264) was a Dominican scholar who wrote a history of the world down to his own time. Stephen I of Hungary (r. 1000–1038), born Vajk, married Gisele of Bavaria, sister of German emperor Henry II, in 996.

100. Correctly book 21 of *Speculum historiale*. Clovis I (r. 481–511) married Clotilde of Burgundy in 492 and later converted to Catholicism.

The Vauderie of Lyon

ANONYMOUS

The text now known as *The Vauderie of Lyon* was, like the *Errors of the Gazarii*, most likely written by an inquisitor in connection with a series of witch trials. Also like the *Errors*, it was originally misdated by several decades. The first and for a long time only known copy was found in a manuscript containing several midcentury cases of witch-craft also described as "vauderie." The most famous of these occurred around the northern French city of Arras in 1459/60.[1] When further copies of *The Vauderie of Lyon* were eventually discovered, however, they provided additional information that proved it was composed at the end of the 1430s.[2]

This redating raises some rich analytical possibilities, but also some problems. The text claims to summarize information from a series of witch trials, but only a few scant records hint at trials around Lyon in this period. Of course, such records could disappear for many reasons. The leading experts on *The Vauderie*, Franck Mercier and Martine Ostorero, speculate that Dominican inquisitors, only recently established in Lyon, used the threat of witchcraft and the emerging notion of horrific sabbaths to bolster their authority. Their efforts, however, largely failed. Unlike other successful inquisitions such as in the diocese of Aosta or Lausanne, the inquisitors in Lyon lacked support from the bishop or other local authorities. No major outbreak of witch-hunting appears to have occurred there.

Despite the failure in this case, witch trials could be a useful mechanism through which new judicial structures might expand

1. Franck Mercier, *La Vauderie d'Arras: Une chasse aux sorcières á l'Automne du Moyen Âge* (Rennes: Presses Universitaire de Rennes, 2006); Gow, Desjardins, and Pageau, *The Arras Witch Treatises.*

2. Mercier and Ostorero, *L'énigme de la Vauderie de Lyon*, 196.

their authority. Thus the efforts of the Lyon inquisitors were probably akin, in their origin, to those of Claude Tholosan working on behalf of the French crown in Dauphiné or Peter of Bern, as described in Johannes Nider's *Anthill*, seeking to extend his city's legal reach into its Alpine hinterland. There may also exist another very direct connection between *The Vauderie of Lyon* and the *Anthill*. In that work, Nider described one of his main sources of information as being "an inquisitor of Autun, who was a zealous reformer in our order's convent in Lyon, and who interrogated many people accused of witchcraft in the diocese of Lyon."[3] If Nider did not simply invent him, then this inquisitor must have been involved in whatever trials were being conducted around Lyon in the late 1430s. Unfortunately, we know nothing more about the man or what form these possible connections may have taken.[4]

In the end, *The Vauderie of Lyon* is again like the *Errors of the Gazarii* in that it is both a richly descriptive and curiously taciturn source. It provides extensive and lurid details about the ghastly activities that supposedly took place at witches' sabbaths, but it only hints at the context in which we should situate and try to understand these descriptions. Perhaps future manuscript discoveries will reveal more clues about its composition and purpose.

The Vauderie of Lyon survives in three known manuscript copies, two in Paris and one in Trier.[5] The first Paris copy, dating from around 1460, was the only copy known to scholarship until the early twenty-first century. The more recently discovered Trier version, dating from 1471, adds significantly to the text. The second Paris copy (Collection Moreau) contains two sections not found in either the first Paris copy or the Trier copy. Although it is by far the latest version in terms of its composition, dating from the seventeenth century, its editors think that it may be closest to the original version of the text.[6]

3. See *Anthill* 5.3.

4. Mercier and Ostorero, *L'énigme de la Vauderie de Lyon*, 210–21.

5. Paris, Bibliothèque nationale de France, MS Lat. 3446, fols. 58r–62r; Trier, Stadtbibliothek, MS 613, fol.

50v–53v; and Paris, Bibliothèque nationale de France, MS Moreau 779, fols. 264r–266r.

6. Mercier and Ostorero, *L'énigme de la Vauderie de Lyon*, 54.

The first Paris copy of the treatise has been edited several times, most famously by Joseph Hansen.[7] I have relied on Mercier and Ostorero's edition, which takes the second Paris copy as its base text. I have followed their practice of including additional material from the Trier copy in the text itself, indicated here by < >. I note other variations, both from the Trier and the first Paris copies, only where they are significant. For ease of identification, I also follow Mercier and Ostorero in labeling the first Paris copy P, the Trier copy T, and the Paris-Moreau copy M.

THE VAUDERIE OF LYON, IN BRIEF[8]

<Articles, in brief summary, concerning the new faithless apostates who are commonly called enchanters.[9]>
Excerpts from certain trials and examinations carried out in the cause of faith concerning a certain horrible and abominable apostasy from the faith or sect that is commonly called *valdesia* <by some> or *faitturerie* <or *fascinerie*> in French, and that, it is revealed, holds sway in the upper parts of this kingdom, for example in Lyon and in the surrounding places and regions.[10]

First, there are in the aforesaid region certain apostates from the faith, both men and women, who are commonly called there, in French, *faicturiers* and *faicturieres* <or *fasciniers* and *fascineres*, so it is said>, who have grown and multiplied into an innumerable number. They have or acquire great familiarity with demons, and they carry out, so it is said, <many> great and grievous <crimes> against the Catholic faith, and strive and work as much as they can to lure Christians into the ruin of damnation.

Indeed, they go out at night, following after Satan—some walking, some riding on a malign spirit that appears to them in some horrible form, others <truly> on a staff. They go to an assembly, sometimes

---

7. Hansen, *Quellen*, 188–95.

8. This title, in French, is found only in P.

9. *Fascinarii*, from the verb *fascinare*, meaning to fascinate or enchant.

10. Although situated in the Rhone River valley, Lyon lies between the Massif Centrale and the Alps, hence in the "upper parts" of the kingdom of France.

quite far away and distant, which among some of them is called, in French, *le Fait*, among others *le Martinet*, but most commonly it is called the synagogue in the vulgar tongue <or the sabbath>.[11]

Also, the devil, cunningly deceiving these wretched people, always presents himself to them visibly in a horrible form, as they themselves confess, sometimes in the form of a very repulsive man, that is, black, completely covered with hair and bristles, with horns, <and also> having a monstrous, drawn out, and twisted shape. He has bulging eyes larger than any animal known to us, flashing <and emitting> flame, and constantly rolling about; a big <long> and crooked nose; exposed ears set high up, emitting <and sending forth> fire; a gaping mouth twisted upward on both sides and extending all the way to his ears; a tongue sticking far out; a chin monstrously stretched and bent back terribly to the other side of his throat; a neck long beyond measure so that it juts out horribly, or too short so that it looks like his head is joined directly to his shoulders; a chest, belly, and other such parts inconceivably deformed. Finally, all along his arms and hands, as well as his legs and feet, hooks and long spines stick out, and the digits of his hands and feet bear terrible claws in the manner of griffins <or bears or lions>. Sometimes, in fact, the demon is accustomed to appear <to them> in the form and likeness of some beast, but always unclean, foul, and extremely vile, such as a goat, fox, large dog, ram, wolf, cat, badger, bull, <bear, monkey,> or something else of this sort, as these perverted people confess.

Also, that malign spirit is accustomed to speak to them in a rough, rasping, dissonant, and dreadful voice, so that whenever he addresses them, they are seized by an incredible terror, and they tremble for a long time afterward in great fear and horror. It is as if they are driven mad, or at least they are drawn into a great and protracted disturbance of the mind and disorder of the imagination.

Also, the staff mentioned above, on which some of these faithless people say and declare that they are borne through the air and also

---

11. *Le Fait* = the event; *le Martinet* = the lash, presumably derived from the punishment the devil inflicted on them. In some cases, the devil or demon presiding over an assembly of witches was known as the Master of the Lash. The addition of *sabbat* in T is one of the earliest known uses of this term, which would come to replace the older "synagogue."

over great distances, should be a specific shape and size, with many notches cut into it, some of which are hidden. And it must be [made] from a specific tree, which should be particularly barren and unfruitful. Otherwise, they assert, it will be useless <for their nefarious task>.

Also, they anoint the aforesaid staff with a certain <fetid, black, and> abominable ointment, directed by the demon's craft and instruction. And, as many of the aforesaid cruel witches have confessed under judicial examination, it must be made from a specific body part of <mainly> unbaptized infants impiously and wickedly killed by them, and in fact sacrificed to their demon, most especially from the heart, which they assert is most suitable and necessary for this diabolical ointment. Thus, as the demon instructs, while making this ointment they utter some words with their filthy mouths, blaspheming and insulting our Redeemer <Jesus Christ> and imploring and revering Satan. These faithless people believe <and say> that the aforesaid staff can perform marvels owing to the power of these [words].

Also, whenever they gather at the synagogue of Satan, these perverse, blind, and wretched people worship that demon, [appearing] in an abominable and fearful form, as described above, as if it were a god. They do this with suppliant prostration and kneeling or genuflection, with clasped and clapping hands, and by kissing that one [the demon] on some part of his body, usually his backside or posterior. <They affirm that during this kiss they smell a very foul odor.>

Also, after the aforesaid impious apostates have done homage, as has been said, with all possible <abasement and> reverence, they give themselves to the demon whom they worship. And some receive that one as their master, others truly and more commonly as their god, promising him under oath that they will not worship or have any other god thereafter.

Also, in this same place they deny the Christian faith and everything pertaining to it, especially holy baptism and all the sacraments of the church, as well as all sacramental items, such as the most holy cross, blessed water, blessed bread, and other things such as these. [And they deny] Christ our redeemer, and the most blessed Virgin Mary, and all the saints of God, and even their place in paradise, not expecting, so they say, any other future happiness or bliss except that which the demon, their god or master, has promised to give them in his paradise.

<Also, certain literate men are found in this execrable sect, who, among other things, have expressly promised to their demon that, whenever they see the chance and can profitably do so, they will secretly exhort or even to some degree publicly proclaim that these disgraceful things do not really take place either in effect or in fact. Rather, they appear only in dreams and fantastical visions, and that it is nothing more than an imaginary delusion. When necessary, they defend and confirm this against those opposing them through ordinary evidence and all possible exhortations.>

Also, when <these idolaters> are detestably denying Christ in the presence of the devil, as described above, they call and name him a false prophet, <Judas,> Jesuel, or some other blasphemous name. Likewise, in their sacrilegious talk they call the blessed Virgin Mary a redheaded whore.

Also, they promise to this same demon, their master, that whenever they find the sacrosanct figure of the cross in a suitable or opportune place, in contempt of our Redeemer they will tread upon it with their feet while uttering the aforesaid blasphemy of "false prophet." <And> wherever they can, they will defile it with their spit and urine and every other kind of filth. Also they will by no means receive blessed water or bread, or keep or preserve it with them or on their persons.

Also, the diabolical synagogue generally occurs in a secluded place far removed from human concourse, and above all at forks <or crossroads>, so they say, or in places where many roads intersect. And yet, so they assert, they cannot be seen by any passersby, but they can see <and hear> any passersby clearly.

Also, at that assembly, immediately after doing homage, as has been described, they begin to dance to the sound of a faint horn or pipes, led by some of these perfidious people themselves, or sometimes by their master the demon. During this dance, at a signal known to them, every man and woman <present there> lies down and mingles together in the manner of brutes or sodomites. And even the devil, as an incubus or succubus, takes whatever man or woman he wishes and has carnal knowledge of them, although brutishly. <And some women from this sect have confessed that the demon often has carnal knowledge of them in a horrible way, appearing to them in the form of a winged beast, either at the assembly or sometimes outside of it.>

Also, at that assembly or synagogue, these same wretched idolaters, as they confess, experience great fear and dread, and even when
they are dancing they are not completely joyful <or carefree>. One
demon presides there, and sometimes there are many, but they are
subservient and obey that one. The demon teaches and instructs
the aforesaid apostates how they should obey and serve him and
not comply with the law and commandments of God, to ignore and
despise everything that pertains to the Christian religion, [and] at his
command to seek and obtain vengeance on those who wrong them
or wish them ill.

Also, they eat and drink while lying in groups on the ground there,
and the meat that they eat is, as they confess, almost raw, slimy, and
filthy, as if it had been dragged through dirt or excrement, and it is
completely tasteless and terrible to eat. Similarly they eat bread there,
but it is heavy, black, and completely devoid of any good flavor. From
a wineskin or bottle, so they say, they drink a certain black, tasteless,
and horrible beverage. And after everyone has had a drink, while
leaving that place they all urinate into this same container, first the
demon and then all these <other> wretches. They affirm and say that
the aforesaid food and drink is found there only through the ministry
and artifice of the demon.

Also, they say that they have a lamp <with black candles> at that
diabolical synagogue, but that it is dim and sort of blackish-green, and
although they often gather there in great numbers, nevertheless they
hardly recognize each other, or they do not recognize each other at
all, with the devil deluding them. And these wretches are not entirely
equal there, but some are more worthy than others, for example those
closer to and more intimate with the devil.

Also, this diabolical assembly usually begins <so they assert>
around sunset or at dusk, and it must always disband, so they say,
before the first rooster crows. Otherwise, after that hour, they can
easily be seen and observed by all. They ascribe the cause of this
dissolution to the fact that everywhere at that hour [bells] are usually rung in churches for the morning service in praise of God, and
Christian religion is stirred to the worship of the Savior, and these
operations <by divine providence> cancel out all the power of the
demon.

Also, they say that [people] from almost any condition or situation are in this damnable sect. In fact [some] come to these assemblies from distant places and far-off regions. And each of them promises that they will seduce as many people as they can and draw them into their depraved apostasy or infidelity.

Also, these impious people promise that, at Easter or other times when they can conveniently do so, when they receive the Eucharist or sacred Host, they will not swallow it but will secretly take it back out of their mouth, keep it hidden in a cloth or paper or other [material], and bring that most sacred Host to the next synagogue for the aforesaid banquet or communal feast. They confess that they most assuredly do this in reality and quite often.[12] When they have taken it there, while the devil sits or stands at a distance, each of these heretics approaches and inflicts every abuse they can on that most sacred Host through shameful contact; for example, by trampling it irreverently with their feet, by vilely defiling it with their spit along with the aforesaid blasphemy about the "false prophet" <and other similar blasphemies>, by pouring urine and their other unspeakable excrements on it with sacrilegious audacity, and moreover by leaving it there amidst every possible disgrace and pollution.

Also, it has been discovered that some of them, at the urging and command of the demon, rear horrible toads over a long period of time, sometimes feeding them the sacred Host that they have taken and secretly kept with them, as described above. Finally, at a certain time set by the demon, they set that toad on fire and incinerate it, and with its ashes they are said to perpetrate and bring about much horrible witchcraft, with the craft and ministry of the devil.

<Also, a few priests of the church have been discovered in this detestable sect and perverse infidelity. When, at the suggestion and command of the demon, they have gone to celebrate a false Mass, they have not consecrated the body and blood of the Lord, but through wicked and damnable intent they have entirely forsaken the sacramental words. And also when managing and administering parish churches, while pretending to baptize, they have scarcely baptized at

12. That they confess to violating the Eucharist "in reality" (*realiter*) is again meant to emphasize that these crimes are not illusory.

all, but [instead] they have presented the essential form of the words with perverse intent or, as has been said, they have omitted [them entirely]. And they have done likewise with the salutary sacrament of penance, as some of them have confessed, and with other ecclesiastical sacraments.>

Also, the aforesaid Satanic assembly is usually held, so they assert, on Thursday nights. And there are each year three or four particular gatherings that are larger than all the others, for example, Holy Thursday, in contempt and reproach, so they say, of the gift of the Lord's Passion; the day of the Lord's Ascension; the feast of Corpus Christi; and the Thursday near the feast of the Nativity of our Lord Jesus Christ.[13] They confess that they do this in mockery of the Christian religion and in clear and express insult to its most holy celebrations and feasts. Many demons assist in these larger assemblies. Although one presides over them, others appear to serve as assistants. And from all over the place these perverse idolaters pour in from many particular [smaller] synagogues to these [larger] ones.

Also, the aforesaid heretics declare and promise to their demon and to each other that they will in no way accuse each other or in any way disclose their witchcraft[14] in court or elsewhere. The devil constantly hardens them so that no mild or friendly exhortation, suggestion, or pure urging can induce them to name and accuse each other, or to be inclined to confess to their crimes. In fact, they are always very hardened <and stubborn in their perfidy>, and however subtle <or diligent> the examination[15] conducted against them, they remain impervious.[16] And when perchance, after much long suffering and various interrogations, they shall have confessed something, nevertheless they are, in the end, wont to change what they have said <and confessed>. Indeed often even after the sentence and injunction

---

13. Holy Thursday is the Thursday before Easter Sunday. The Feast of the Ascension occurs on the Thursday thirty-nine days after Easter. The feast of Corpus Christi occurs on a Thursday in June or occasionally in late May. The Nativity of Christ (Christmas) is a nonmoveable feast, always falling on December 25.

14. Here *maleficia* might be better translated as "wicked deeds" or "crimes," although the implication would be crimes done through magic.

15. P adds "or thorough the inquiry and torture."

16. P adds "and they do not want to confess the truth about themselves or their other accomplices."

have been carried out against them and they have undertaken penance, they are accustomed to take back <and foreswear> entirely everything <proffered and asserted against them> that they had confessed and repeatedly affirmed.

Also, these criminals are generally led into this error and horror by desire for, and under pretense of, riches, luxuries, and honors, although often they are found to be poor, destitute, and extremely needy, because these things had been promised by him who from the beginning stood not in the truth, and whose father is a lie. Granted that some of them testify that they have sometimes received from him, as if in salary, a little money, but it is false and of little value, <and nothing with a cross imprinted on it. They say that they do not often bring back profit or gain; in fact, when the assembly disperses, that [money received there] is immediately reduced or converted into coal or rocks or something else of no value.>

<Also, each of the aforesaid infidels typically has their own familiar and special demon, whom they call upon by invoking it by a specific and explicit name whenever they want, and immediately that devil, as if bound by some action, reveals itself in different forms, by transforming in turn now in this way, now in that. Moreover, many of these perfidious people say that they are sometimes subject to a single demon as if to a master and serve it in particular.>

Also, very often, on account of their desire for and pursuit of vengeance against their enemies, they are led to a nefarious crime of this sort, whence at the devil's urging and instruction they carry out and cause some <poisonings [and] illusions > suited to every kind of witchcraft, by which they cause sickness in both people and animals, feebleness, and death, as well as inclement weather. With powders made through the demon's craft, which they secretly spread about and put in food and drink, they inflict various grave ailments; indeed, often deadly or long-lasting illnesses. They often cause abortions in pregnant women by means of a crafty touch or by doing some superstitious thing, or, as it is said, by deceitfully adding something in their drink or food. In fact, often they cruelly smother children they are delivering from their mother's womb in the manner of midwives, <most often before the cleansing of baptism, if they can,> or others lying in a bed, crib, or in their mother's lap, by touching them secretly and imperceptibly.

Moreover, some do many evil things through herbs designated expressly by the demon for such witchcraft. They gather these at a particular time and with the superstitious observance of prescribed words, signs, gestures, <times,> and places, and they administer them to people and animals on whom they intend to inflict witchcraft while expressly invoking their master the demon. Some do many evil things by means of ointments made with diabolical craft from a horrible concoction. Others inflict the aforesaid witchcraft, illnesses, and ailments through needles, pins, or nails; that is, they prick some lead or wax image, or something of this sort, with the needle, pin, or nail in that part in which they likewise want to harm the intended person or animal, uttering certain diabolical words while they are pricking it. Immediately that person or animal feels themselves to be pierced by the sharp pain of sickness, however distant or far away from the place they are. And the more deeply the needle, pin, or nail is pressed in, the more intense the pain grows and the person <more violently> suffers; <but> conversely, however much it is drawn back out, the pain immediately eases and diminishes. And they assert that they can achieve the same [effect] if they prick a tree, especially one that is barren, or any kind of <dry> wood <with the observances set out above>.

<Also, the infirmities that these witches inflict and cause are prolonged and last as long as they want. They are generally not continuous, however, but last for only a few days at a time. They afflict and torture the bewitched people through stabbing pains and very sharp stings. First terrible afflictions begin in the joints of the hands and feet and the other extremities of the body, and then they progress to the entrails, causing intolerable suffering until people are afflicted by near-complete dehydration and desiccation, which unnaturally shortens their lives. And the qualities and conditions of these illnesses are so marvelous and strange that not even the most experienced physician can perceive or recognize clear signs or symptoms of them, and so he cannot administer the most effective remedy. Other people of this sort have been discovered who, by superstitiously gazing into a mirror placed in water or by some other execrable means of divination, can discern

and clearly describe the nature of the sickness and the singular quality of the perpetrator of that crime.>

<Also, it has been found that some of these criminals receive and possess only [the ability] to inflict witchcraft, but not to remove it. Others, and in fact the majority of them, [can do] both, that is, inflict and afterward remove [witchcraft]. And there are some who receive and obtain power from the demon only provisionally and for just one occasion, but there are others who receive it permanently.>

<Also, it has been discovered through their confession that there are women among them who, whenever they want, deprive wet nurses who live near them of milk, no matter how abundant it would seem to be. Likewise they confess that they cause their neighbors' cows, goats, and other livestock to dry up, drawing the milk away from them and collecting it into their own breasts secretly and by superstitious means. On account of this, they inflict much harm and injury on their neighbors. They assert that this is generally done in this way. On certain days very early in the morning they go walking openly through a verdant meadow, drawing after them a linen cloth and at specified times uttering certain words given [to them] by the demon. They proceed unhooded, with unbound hair and bare feet, carrying in their hands toads in a pot into which they have put a little milk, and addressing them with certain words. And they encircle and walk around that meadow while observing other wonders or illusions all around them.>

Also, through the aforesaid pestiferous means—namely, powders, herbs, ointments, words, needles, pins, nails, and things like that—they very often stir up hatred and discontent between spouses, however much each loves the other, so that these couples are unable to live together, but rather they flee from one another for as long as the witches wish. Moreover, through this same witchcraft they cause all the livestock of those whom they hate to languish and die, and they infect springs and drinking water with the aforesaid poisons, causing both people and livestock to die. Indeed, as they have sometimes confessed, while casting these diabolical poisons into springs, ponds, and rivers, they are accustomed to cause storms in the air, such that the fields of those whom they hate, along with their vineyards and fruit trees, are destroyed and ruined with great precision, while others around them remain unharmed and intact, as has been demonstrated by experience.

Also, they assert that some of them can cause the milk from their cows or cattle to increase by drawing it away from their neighbors' livestock and bringing it to their own through superstitious art. In order to do this, so they say, at a certain time they draw a cloth or towel across their property while uttering suspicious words in order to collect dew. Then they give this to their cattle to drink.

Also, many of them say that they can confine and hold sheep and cows, goats, kids, and other animals in some park, meadow, or nonenclosed field—according to them [this is called] *enserer* in French[17]—so that they cannot go out unless the witches should wish it, nor would a wolf or other predator be able to get in or harm them in any way.[18]

Also, in clear and explicit evidence of the fee[19] and homage owed, and of servitude promised, these impious idolaters deliver without fail to the devil their master some tribute of wheat, barley, oats, rye, millet, eggs, <chickens, hens, whatever sort of animal,> and other things of this sort, generally once a month or at certain times during the year, and in a certain place designated by the demon. If they fail in this or any other obligations, they are severely punished and whipped by the demon.

Also, they admit and confess that during the night, following behind a demon who leads them and opens doors for them, they secretly and silently enter cellars and storerooms, and draw wine out of the barrels and drink it in great quantities. Then, after they have done this, first the demon and then all these wretched idolaters climb up on the same barrel from which they drank and one by one they urinate in it and try to fill the vessel up again with their filth. They assert that they [can] see each other there via a dim light provided by the demon, although they are imperceptible to others, and they can be neither seen nor heard.

Also, these malicious and perverse apostates strive to lead simple people, and especially young people who have not yet been well instructed or trained in faith, into this damnable sect, and unfortunately they do bring in [many] throughout the regions mentioned above.

17. To grip/hold tightly.

18. The two preceding sections ("Also, they assert . . . harm them in any way.") are found only in M.

19. *census*, here in the sense of a fixed payment or obligation that tenants or serfs would owe to their lords.

After they have been bound to this sect, despite frequent sermons, constant threats, and even the constant experience of [seeing] those who have been burned in fire, nevertheless throughout their lives these stubborn people persist <and continue> unshakably in their error and execrable horror, some for thirty years, some for forty, and others for fifty years or even longer.

Also, during the Easter holidays when <some of them, perhaps, but indeed [only] a few> come to confession, driven more by fear and shame than by contrition or penitence, they either reveal nothing about these sort of crimes, or if by chance they should reveal something, nevertheless with the demon <impelling or> frightening or <cleverly> urging them into it, they are not afraid to relapse immediately.

<Also, one must not think from what has been set out above that every one of these perfidious people do and commit everything recounted here, although many of them or even the majority of them do so. And there are also certain other things that are accomplished in part through deliberate purpose, but in part owing to the ignorance of these perfidious people, not to mention the experiences they have had. These are, nevertheless, the ones that are found more evidently and commonly among them.>

Also, these perfidious people show signs of their impiety by which they can be distinguished from true Catholics, such as that they rarely if ever go to church, even on feast days, but <instead> they deliberately go away somewhere on worldly business. Indeed, if they sometimes go [to church] by way of pretense, nevertheless they hardly behave like faithful Catholics, for they reject holy water by scattering it around themselves,[20] and they do not know how to cross themselves properly. Instead they feign crossing themselves with a circle or in some other improper way. They do not generally <very often> know the Lord's Prayer, Hail Mary, or the statement of faith contained in the Creed. They secretly draw the sign of the cross on the ground, and when no one is looking they spit [on it]. If they falsely receive blessed bread to eat, they spit it back out. They do not look upon the most holy body of Christ when it is consecrated on the altar and elevated by a priest, but they turn their eyes elsewhere. And if they are being watched

20. As opposed to on themselves.

attentively and fixedly by priests and religious men they immediately blush and, rolling their eyes all about, they show clearly enough that they are aware of their crimes. <They hold the bonds of excommunication in contempt, and they are not afraid to remain entangled in them for many years. [But] they fear the arrival of inquisitors above all else, [and] as soon as they draw near to some place, they [the witches] immediately flee and seek hiding places.>

These things and much more besides are found in the confessions of these <perfidious people> when examined by inquisitors, but insofar as we have been able, favoring brevity and so that things should not get tedious, we have summarized them briefly. Since these things are wicked to the highest degree—indeed they should be regarded as more dangerous than any other earlier heresies <in the past>, and more ruinous to the Catholic faith—it is rightly necessary that we exert ourselves in order to uproot and destroy this extremely criminal apostasy <and impious infidelity>, lest it should spread and grow even further. Which indeed [is the conclusion to which] this very difficult matter clearly leads.[21]

<These things, however, must not be divulged or explained in any detail heedlessly to simpleminded or fragile people, since the bare and reckless explication of such obscenity and foulness could be more harmful than beneficial to the feebleminded. For the allure of wickedness imprudently adduced and disclosed often attracts and perversely disturbs the calm and sobriety of the soul. But indeed it is necessary that these things should be revealed to wise and morally irreproachable people, in order to seek their advice and assistance.>

21. T reads here: "Which rightly [is the conclusion that] this difficult matter has exposed completely, and [to which] it clearly leads."

A Pair of Fifteenth-Century Trials

The aim of this volume has been to bring together and present to an English-speaking audience the earliest known descriptions of conspiratorial witchcraft and the sabbath as contained in a set of works composed by lay and clerical officials in the 1430s. Each of those men, however, was either involved in or at least cognizant of trials for witchcraft conducted at this time, from which reports of conspiratorial activities emerged. To give readers some sense of this other kind of historical source, I include here records from two trials that are each connected to one of the sources above. Jubertus, a sixty-year-old furrier from Bavaria, was tried in Briançon by Claude Tholosan.[1] The trial of Aymonet Maugetaz, with its notable description of witches breaking up sheets of ice on mountain peaks in order to make hail, may have informed the expanded version of the *Errors of the Gazarii* now held in Basel.[2]

Trial records do not necessarily represent a more direct source of information about beliefs surrounding witchcraft and the sabbath. They were just as heavily constructed as the reports and treatises translated above. They also represent summaries of longer processes. The source for Jubertus, for example, records only his final sentencing after a trial lasting seventeen days. Even where the texts appear to give direct quotes from the accused, we must remember that these were Latin documents summarizing interrogations that took place in the vernacular, and of course considerable pressure could be brought to bear on the accused to produce a particular kind of confession.

The two cases presented here are also each atypical in certain ways. Jubertus was an old man who had traveled widely, perhaps owing to his profession as a dealer in animal skins.[3] Having apparently

---

1. See Paravy, *De la chrétienté romaine a la Réforme en Dauphiné*, 2:814–16.

2. Ostorero et al., *Imaginaire*, 341–42.

become involved in what appears to be more learned forms of demonic magic in Bavaria and Austria, he had the misfortune to be apprehended in Dauphiné during a witch hunt. The description of his membership in a sect that would meet regularly at "the usual place" is actually quite brief.

Aymonet was perhaps a bit more usual sort of suspect—a local boy from a supposed lineage of witches, brought into the sect by his father. His interrogation was part of a series of trials just beginning in the Swiss region of Vaud, along the north shore of Lake Geneva, conducted mainly by Dominican inquisitors based in Lausanne.[4] What makes Aymonet (somewhat) unusual is that he voluntarily came before the inquisitor Ulric de Torrente, and since he freely repented, he was released without punishment. Despite the voluntary nature of this confession, we must be cognizant of the fact that someone seeking pardon was probably inclined to tell the inquisitor things that he wanted or expected to hear.

The trial record for Jubertus is found in Grenoble, in the same manuscript that contains Claude Tholosan's treatise.[5] I have followed the edition by Joseph Hansen.[6] There has previously been both a partial and full English translation.[7] The trial record for Aymonet Maugetaz is found in the archives of the canton of Vaud just outside Lausanne.[8] It has been edited, along with a French translation, by Martine Ostorero in *L'imaginaire du sabbat*.[9]

3. Paravy, *De la chrétienté romaine a la Réforme en Dauphiné*, 2:814.

4. On these trials, see Bernard Andenmatten and Kathrin Utz Tremp, "De l'hérésie à la sorcellerie: L'inquisiteur Ulric de Torrenté (vers 1420–1445) et l'affermissement de l'inquisition en Suisse romande," *Zeitschrift für Schweizerische Kirchengeschichte* 86 (1992): 69–119; Utz Tremp, *Von der Häresie zur Hexerei*, 535–53.

5. Archives Départmentales de l'Isère, B 4356, fol. 222r–226v.

6. Hansen, *Quellen*, 539–44.

7. Kieckhefer, *Forbidden Rites*, 30–32; Maxwell-Stuart, *Witch Beliefs and Witch Trials*, 190–95.

8. Archives Cantonales Vaudoises, Ac 29, pp. 1–3.

9. Ostorero et al., *Imaginaire*, 344–53.

THE TRIAL OF JUBERTUS OF BAVARIA

In the name of the Lord, amen. In the year of the birth of our Lord 1437 and on November 28 in Briançon, in the place recorded below, in the presence of the noble and wise man Constant Borchard, the Dauphin's fiscal procurator in Briançon, in the name of the Dauphin, Jubertus of Bavaria, from the city of Regensburg in lower Germany, a furrier by trade, was consigned to hear final sentence, in brief and peremptory fashion, concerning certain criminal proceedings done and directed by the Dauphin's superior court in Briançon against the aforesaid accused, Jubertus, in accordance with the duties of that court, by instruction of the lord fiscal procurator, as established by the records of the case and proceedings concerning that consignment.

On that day, and in the place designated above, the aforesaid lord fiscal procurator appeared before the noble, circumspect man, Lord Claude Tholosan, licensed in law, adviser to the Dauphin, chief magistrate of Briançon, requesting and requiring, in the Dauphin's name, that in the said interrogatory process titles and cases be determined and sentence be carried out on behalf of the fiscal office,[10] and the aforesaid accused be condemned, corrected, and punished according to and in accordance with what is demanded by the transgressions and crimes perpetrated by the accused, in order to provide an example for other perpetrators of such heinous transgressions.

The said Jubertus appeared, asking that mercy be shown to him and that he be treated mercifully. And the lord judge, having heard the aforesaid parties appearing in his court, proceeded to the final sentence as follows.

We, Claude Tholosan, the aforesaid magistrate, saw and considered how the accused, Jubertus, was charged with sorcery and certain magical acts, and also [we considered] previous reports and judgments. He had been brought into the Dauphin's castle in Briançon and was questioned and interrogated there by us. Then he was examined by many others at various times about this same sorcery and witchcraft.

---

10. As described in the introduction to Tholosan's *So That the Errors of Magicians and Witches* . . . above, witchcraft was regarded as a form of treason, and in Roman law, which had been revived in France at this time, the fiscal office or treasury had jurisdiction over cases of treason.

Finally, we considered the said interrogatory process that we had conducted and directed against the accused Jubertus, as required by our office. The tenor of the allegations to which that same Jubertus confessed and their course is as follows.

First, the said Jubertus said and confessed by his own free oath, by the touch of his hand.[11] When the interrogation ceased,[12] he voluntarily declared that it was true that he was sixty years old, and that for more than ten years he had served a powerful man in Bavaria who was called John Cunalis, a priest and rector in the city called Munich in the aforesaid [region of] Bavaria, near Bohemia.

Also, he further said and confessed that the said John Cunalis had a book of necromancy, and when he who spoke [Jubertus] opened the said book, immediately there were three demons who appeared to him, one of whom was called Lustful, another Prideful, and another Greedy. And the first appeared to him in the form of a pleasing young woman, twelve years old, who slept with him at night, and he was charmed [by her] and had a pleasurable experience.

Also, he would worship that devil [Lustful] like a god at night, bending his knees and then turning his ass toward the sunrise, and he would make a cross in the dirt and spit on it three times, and step on it three times with his left foot, and urinate and defecate [on it], and wherever he saw a cross, he would spit at it and deny God three times.

Also, at dawn he would worship Prideful in the same way, who first appeared in the form of a mole, then in the form of a middle-aged man clothed in black garments. And Greedy appeared to him at the hour of compline[13] in the form of an old man clothed in filthy garments, and he carried a purse full of money. And he [Jubertus] would worship him as above and offer him everything that he acquired on feast days.

Also, he would give to Prideful his leftovers when he ate and drank, and he would give three or five pennies to Lustful on Holy Friday before Easter, and he likewise gave his limbs and body, and his soul after death. And the said devils wanted him to deny God, whom

---

11. I.e., placing his hand on some holy object while he swore.

12. Standard inquisitorial procedure was to interrogate suspects, often under torture or the threat of torture,

and then require them to "voluntarily" reconfirm what they had said.

13. Evening prayers performed before retiring for the night.

they call the cursed prophet, and when he would worship these three demons like gods, he would turn his face toward the sunset and his ass toward the sunrise, saying what he said. And when he partook of Lustful,[14] the others would mock him.

Also, he further said and confessed that the devil Greedy, one of his masters, once gave him three ducats from a hidden store of money and urged him to kill himself.

Also, he further said that when he went through the streets and was with the demons, and he came upon a cross, the devils would flee from it and they would make a great circuit [around it]. And they would also forbid him to do good, to worship the sacred Host, and to close his eyes while it was elevated.[15] And they would forbid him to receive holy water and to kiss the cross and the pax,[16] asserting that they alone were all-powerful gods.

Also, he further said and confessed that on Sunday the seventeenth of the present month, all three demons were with him in prison. Their eyes shone like sulfurous fire. They said to the accused that they would have protected him if he had not revealed what is set out above. And then he partook of and joined carnally with the aforesaid Lustful. Moreover, he said that these demons would have freed him from prison if he had not revealed what is set out above.

Also, he further said and confessed that these devils then said to him that he would be interrogated very exactingly the next day, and that he would be required to tell the whole truth, and that he would then be put to death. By certain signs they revealed to him the person who had been sent to do this.

Also, he further said and confessed that once he went with his master through some woods.[17] They were attacked there by brigands, who were turned away in flight by a multitude of devils appearing in the form of armed men. Moreover, he asserted that the world is full

---

14. I.e., had sex with the demon.

15. Since the congregation was expected to view the elevated Host, the intended meaning is almost certainly that the demons forced him to close his eyes at this moment, rather than forbidding it.

16. The pax was a liturgical object used by the congregation when exchanging the "kiss of peace" during a Mass.

17. Although above he refers to the three demons as his masters, here he seems to mean John Cunalis.

of people who invoke demons, and that these devils attend to them eagerly, mainly because the world is filled with sin, wars, and divisions.

Also, he further said and confessed that his master, with the aid of demons, caused a bridge to be built in one night over a certain river in Bavaria, in a place called Saint Mary the Hermit.[18]

Also, he further said and confessed that, because she had displeased him, he had proposed blinding Jeanne, the widow of John the Rustic of the present place,[19] by drawing her figure with two keys in a manner and form described in the trial. He drew that image on Sunday below the name[s] of the devils, with materials and in a manner described in the trial. He did likewise to someone called John the Craftsman of Vienna in the duchy of Austria. He had revealed the things described above before his arrest, and he had boasted about how he did it.

Also, he further said and confessed that he is a necromancer and that, with his devils, he invisibly seized a certain child for his master in the city of Munich. They also seized a certain child in its cradle, whom they killed and roasted and mixed with the blood from the corpse of a child who died without being baptized, [also] mixing in nocturnal pollutions, menstrual blood, and female pubic hair, as it is the custom of necromancers to do. They raise up unhappy children who are demons,[20] and put them in the place of children [they have] carried off, in order to deceive their parents. These children appear to be the original children, but they have a swollen stomach and a big head, and they are always crying. And they return when they want to,[21] as he saw and experienced in Germany.

Also, he further said and confessed that what is described above happens to those who put their children in cradles without a cross or blessing.

---

18. Paravy, *De la chrétienté romaine a la Réforme en Dauphiné*, 2:815n4, suggests a connection to the Benedictine abbey of "Our Lady of the Hermits" at Einsiedeln, Switzerland, which was dedicated to the Virgin Mary. Saint Mary the Hermit could also refer to the fifth-century saint Mary of Egypt, however, who was the focus of widespread devotion in this period. My thanks to James Mixson and Miri Rubin for consulting on this matter.

19. I.e., Briançon.

20. The verb *suscitare* often conveys the sense of raising the dead. Here it means raising demonic changelings up from the netherworld.

21. I.e., to the netherworld.

Also, he further said and confessed that this happened on Thursday and Saturday nights, when he and others of the sect were carried to the usual place in the blink of an eye upon [a pile of] mule or horse dung, by the ministration of devils. In that place they delivered accounts of their wicked deeds to demons along with others of the sect, and whoever had committed more witchcraft was commended more by the devil and would sit in the devil's place. And there they were taught to commit more wretched evils, as well as in what situations these should be committed.

Also, he further said and confessed that about two years ago he was in Vienna, a city in Austria, on the fifth day of the week, that is a Thursday, and there were three drunk cooks there in a certain tavern who had refused to give him a drink. And when it was late, as they were leaving, one of them said to the other two, "get up, in the name of the devil, and let me pass." And immediately outside the door, at the accused's request, all three of his master's demons seized those three, and they threw one into a well, another into the cesspool or toilet of the Preachers, and another into the toilet of the Friars Minor.[22] Of these, only the one who had been thrown into the well was killed, as the others were rescued by the friars at dawn.

Also, he further said and confessed that they made poisons with the help of the devils, through which they can kill people, either suddenly with the help of demons or by a slow languishing, according to the wish of whoever administers it [the poison]. And poisons [made] from a basilisk, toad, snake, spider, or scorpion are administered, to a greater or lesser degree in the name of the devil, in a manner and form contained in the trial.

Also, he further said that he gave some of the said poison in a small dish to someone called Conrad in the city of Munich in Bavaria.

Also, he further said and confessed that when he went through the streets and saw images of the Virgin Mary or a cross, he would spit at them three times in disdain of the Father, Son, and Holy Spirit, and that on the feast day of Saint John the Baptist[23] he would gather certain herbs named in the trial as medicines. And he would first worship

22. Preachers = Dominicans; Friars   23. June 24.
Minor = Franciscans.

them on bended knees and pull them out [of the ground] in the name of his devils and in disdain of almighty God, the creator of all things.

Also, he further said that the devils urged him to commit lustful acts, which greatly please them, and perpetrate rape, and commit all kinds of wicked acts. And they called the cross a crippled and shameful piece of wood. And that when he went wandering through the world, with the aid of the devils he would recognize those [members] of this sect and infidelity by the smoke from their stoves, in a manner and form described in the trial.

Also, that he confessed the things set out above freely and repeatedly in court, and he asserted on his oath that they were true. Moreover, he had been overwhelmed by the evidence [again him].

Also, from what is set out above it is apparent that the accused is and was for a long time a necromancer, witch, diviner, poisoner, apostate, murderer, invoker of demons, and astrologer.

We have seen above the numerous reiterations made by the said accused described in the trial, and we have seen how the said accused freely persisted in his aforesaid confessions, and how he persevered steadfastly in what he said. And finally we have seen and ruminated on the legal proceedings made and brought against the accused, and we have diligently observed and met with him. We have also seen and heard each and every thing that the said parties wanted to say and set forth at this day and hour, appointed and established by us for them to hear our final sentence. The procedure for recanting has been held in this case, and the trial has been concluded and made public. We sit in court with both experts and books.[24] By sacred custom, holy scripture has been placed in our sight, so that our judgment should be made correctly in the face of God and our eyes should always see impartially in these and all other matters, inclining no more to one side than another, but weighing this kind of case with balanced deliberation and equal measure. We first invoke the name of Christ [our] God, and protect ourselves with the sign of the venerable holy cross, and say, "in the name of the Father and Son and Holy Spirit, amen." By what we saw and gathered in the course of the trial and things stemming from

24. I.e., legal experts and texts that the judge has consulted.

it, which disturb us [greatly] and can and should disturb the mind of anyone judging properly, through this our final sentence, which we utter from our own mouth, we state, pronounce, decree, declare, and issue judgment as follows.

Since in the course of this trial it is completely certain and sufficiently apparent to us, the aforesaid judge, through the said accused's own frequent, consistent confession made on his own bodily oath, that the accused detestably committed and perpetrated the things described above with deliberate purpose and stubborn mind, that he is a magician and witch, and consequently, in whatever part of the world he may be, he is an enemy of God and humanity, therefore in many ways, and by both divine and human judgment, he has incurred the penalty of the ultimate punishment. We cannot shut our eyes and ignore this without serious offence to almighty God and reprisals from both God and the minister of the law, and in our zeal for justice we cannot let these things go unpunished. Therefore through this our final sentence, which we pronounce in these present documents from our own mouth, we condemn the said accused, that in the place ordained by us and regularly used for the execution of justice he should publicly be burned alive on a pile of wood erected there and consumed by devouring flame. By the same sentence we confiscate and seize his goods for the Dauphin's fiscal office and treasury, so that he might provide an example to others wishing to do similar things. We commit to the noble castellan of Briançon or his deputy the execution of our present sentence, which we should ultimately certify in a public document, as is proper.

The present sentence was made, read out, and published in the year and on the day [given] above, within the courthouse at Briançon, in the presence of the noble Humbert of Névache, Reynand Rainlis, Gonet Durand, Jean Medici of Briançon, Ponezon Scrivian of Queyras, and many others.[25]

M. Sager, notary.

---

25. Névache and Queyras are localities just north and south of Briançon.

THE TRIAL OF AYMONET MAUGETAZ OF EPESSES

Let all those present and in the future know that in the current year 1438, on July 30, Aymonet, son of the late Jaquet Maugetaz, also called Cossandeir, resident of Epesses,[26] long since convicted of heresy and burned by a secular court, appeared voluntarily and presented himself before the venerable brother Ulric de Torrente of the Order of Preachers,[27] master of the sacred page, inquisitor of heretics, without having been accused of heresy, or summoned, or admonished, and also in my presence, the undersigned judicial officer.[28] Which Aymonet, being about twenty years old, with great tears and repeated sobs and sighs, humbly and devoutly asked the aforesaid lord inquisitor to absolve him of many grave and heinous sins that he had committed in the sect of the heretics with his late father.

He confessed his sins in the following way in court before me, the undersigned judicial officer; namely, that five years ago his father wanted him to go to a certain meadow where he would deny God. But he did not want to go there, and he stayed the whole day with some children guarding the horses and, when evening came, he went home, [where] his father beat him violently because he had not gone to the meadow.

Finally one night his father made him go with him. As he made his way near Epesses, his father mounted on a small black ox or black foal—he could not discern clearly what it was—and his father made him mount behind [him] on the said animal, and they began to go, and they went so vigorously and violently that it was a wonder.[29] But he could not really say where they had gone, except that those who were there told him that they were near Basel.[30] And there they met many kinds of people,[31] and he thinks that there were more than a hundred, both men and women. And a certain black man came there, who was

26. A community a few miles east of Lausanne.

27. The Dominican inquisitor in Lausanne from 1420 to 1440.

28. *Juratus*, literally a sworn individual, in this context a municipal official.

29. I.e., it was a hair-raising ride.

30. About one hundred miles north of Lausanne.

31. The Latin *gentes* implies different "nations," i.e., people from different regions; given Basel's location, perhaps both German- and French-speaking. See note 35 below.

the devil, and he said to Aymonet that he required him to deny God
and that he should take him [the devil] as his god. He did so, and he
denied the entire Trinity and holy baptism and whatever comes from
that. Later he [the devil] transformed himself into the likeness of a
great black lampstand with an opening in its back, and later still he
transformed himself into the form of a black cat, and everyone who
was there came and kissed him on his ass. And he [Aymonet] did this
like the others. And the devil gave him five shillings, but he does not
remember what became of them. And after all these things had been
done, they ate and drank there, and his father brought him bread and
a scrap of meat, but he did not know what kind of meat it was. And
he said that he signed himself,[32] and immediately he fell a long way
and did not know where he was, in some meadow. But soon someone
arrived who came looking for him and brought him back to the place
where he was before.

And the aforesaid Aymonet said that at the society there were
many candles that gave off a light or flame called *blovaz* in French.[33]
And after they had worshiped [the devil], all the people, both men and
women, began to mingle with one another and to cohabitate,[34] one
with the other, just like dogs.

Asked how the women positioned themselves, he said and showed
that they put their hands on the ground and the men placed themselves
above their posterior.

Asked if he did this, he said yes, with some woman whom he did
not know.

Asked how the devil directed them concerning the body of Christ,
he said that he directed that when he [Aymonet] took it from a priest,
he should not swallow it but put his left hand to his mouth and keep
it in a napkin, and that later he should take it with him to the devil.

Asked how many times he received the body of Christ, he said
twice.

Asked if he did as he [the devil] said, he said no, instead he did as
the curate directed, who directed that one should not touch the body

32. I.e., he made the sign of the
cross.

33. I.e., they gave off a blue light.

34. Presumably Aymonet used a
vernacular euphemism for sex that the
scribe tried to replicate in Latin via
cohabitare.

of Christ with the teeth but only with the tongue. Therefore when he came to the Easter feast, when he had received the body of Christ, he replied that he had eaten it. His father threatened him and said to him, "you are nothing but a liar and you do not keep your promises." And he said many other things to him.

Also, asked what the devil directed concerning blessed bread, he said that he directed that one might well take it from a priest, but one should not eat it. Instead one should trample it under foot and then give it to a dog.

Also, asked about holy water, he said that he [the devil] directed that one should not sprinkle it on oneself but behind oneself.

Also, asked what he directed concerning confession, he said that he directed that one might well confess, but not that one had denied God or that one had received the devil as god, and so forth.

Asked and admonished to say if he knew any people in the said society, and to name them, he said no, other than the woman called Rufa de Valle, who was there then. But he did not know any others, and indeed he did not understand much that they said.[35]

Also, he said that another time he was at the sect or society with his father, as above, on a certain mountain behind Gruyeres, although he did not know its name.[36] There they met some other men who broke big chunks of ice with pointed iron hammers, which the devil provided. And there was a great big black man there with hyssop or an aspergillum who cast water over the ice and it froze back together.[37] But he, the deponent [Aymonet], did nothing to help with this breaking. Instead he watched over the animal on which they had come. And later a large cloud came, shadowy and black, which lifted all the ice into the air. And the deponent mounted the animal on which he and his father had come, and he returned and was in front of his father's house. And the devil appeared in their parish in the likeness of his father with other people signaling the time.[38] And the deponent added

35. Perhaps meaning that most of the attendees spoke other languages, or at least other dialects.

36. Gruyeres is in a mountainous region about twenty miles east of Lausanne.

37. Hyssop is a plant, the twigs of which were used to cast holy water; an aspergillum is a bristled brush used for the same purpose.

38. Most likely by ringing a bell.

that, insofar as he knows, he signaled the time willingly. And he said that his father had remained with the other people who had broken the ice, and they had carried the aforesaid ice and hail over Vevey, and they had caused a storm over Vevey.[39]

Asked what day this was, he said that it was a Tuesday, early in the morning, about the hour of prime.[40]

Afterward, he said that another time his father took him near the Rhone, where the Rhone enters the lake,[41] and his father wanted the deponent to take a child from a certain house, but he refused. And then his father and some other ones who were there entered the house and seized or killed the child; he did not really know what they did there.

Also, he said that the first time [at the assembly], when he was near Basel, the devil wanted him to offer him his body or soul, but he refused to do so. And then his father said to the devil, "he will do it another time." And then when they had been [there] three times, he offered him the little finger of his left hand when he was dead.

Also, he said that only three weeks ago he, the deponent and confessant, went from the village of Epesses to help the curate of Cully,[42] and the devil appeared to him in the form of a small hare and said to him, "you do not keep to that which you promised me. Why do you not keep to this?" The deponent responded to him, "I will not keep to anything with you. Instead I reject you completely and do not want to have anything to do with you." And then the hare disappeared when the deponent and confessant made the sign of the cross.

And this was what the aforesaid Aymonet confessed of his own free will. And then the said inquisitor ordered and appointed me, the undersigned judicial officer, [to go] with the said confessant to the venerable and cautious man, the lord cantor of Lausanne, vicar of the reverend father and lord in Christ, the lord John, bishop of Lausanne, to obtain sacramental absolution for the said Aymonet. I, the undersigned judicial officer, led that Aymonet to the said lord cantor,

---

39. Vevey is about ten miles southwest of Gruyeres and five miles east of Epesses on Lake Geneva.

40. I.e., daybreak.

41. The Rhone enters Lake Geneva along its southeastern shore, roughly across from Vevey on the northern shore.

42. Less than a mile west of Epesses.

and, when absolution had been received, I brought the same Aymonet back to the said lord inquisitor who, in my presence as before, and in the presence of the undersigned witnesses, made this same Aymonet abjure the said heresy and sect completely, as well as everything stemming from it, under penalty of law, saying to this same Aymonet that, whereas he had come voluntarily, this first time holy mother church would spare him entirely. But he should take care that he should not return any more to that heresy, otherwise they would proceed against him according to the form of the law. On bended knees and with both hands on God's holy gospels, Aymonet swore that he would never return to that heresy and sect.

And the aforesaid was done in my presence, the undersigned judicial officer, and in the presence of the brothers Raymond and Aymon Cerjat of the Order of Preachers of Lausanne, in the chamber of the lord inquisitor in the convent of the Friars Preachers, in the year and on the day that [are given] above.

Signed by Peter Por . . . to

SELECTED BIBLIOGRAPHY

Ammann-Doubliez, Chantal. "Les chasses aux sorciers vues sous un angle politique: Pouvoirs et persécutions dans le diocèse de Sion au XVe siècle." In *Chasse aux sorcières et démonologie: Entre discours et pratiques (XIVe–XVIIe siècles)*, edited by Martine Ostorero, Georg Modestin, and Kathrin Utz Tremp, 5–25. Micrologus' Library 36. Florence: SISMEL, 2010.

Bailey, Michael D. *Battling Demons: Witchcraft, Heresy, and Reform in the Late Middle Ages*. University Park: Pennsylvania State University Press, 2003.

———. "Diabolic Magic." In *The Cambridge History of Magic and Witchcraft in the West: From Antiquity to the Present*, edited by David J. Collins, 361–92. Cambridge: Cambridge University Press, 2015.

———. "The Feminization of Magic and the Emerging Idea of the Female Witch in the Late Middle Ages." *Essays in Medieval Studies* 19 (2002): 120–34.

———. "From Sorcery to Witchcraft: Clerical Conceptions of Magic in the Later Middle Ages." *Speculum* 76 (2001): 960–90.

———. "The Medieval Concept of the Witches' Sabbath." *Exemplaria* 8 (1996): 419–39.

Bailey, Michael D., and Edward Peters. "A Sabbat of Demonologists: Basel, 1431–1440." *The Historian* 65 (2003): 1375–95.

Blauert, Andreas. *Frühe Hexenverfolgungen: Ketzer-, Zauberei- und Hexenprozesse des 15. Jahrhunderts*. Hamburg: Junius, 1989.

Blécourt, Willem de. "Sabbath Stories: Toward a New History of Witches' Assemblies." In *The Oxford Handbook of Witchcraft in Early Modern Europe and Colonial America*, edited by Brian P. Levack, 84–100. Oxford: Oxford University Press, 2013.

Borst, Arno. "The Origins of the Witch-Craze in the Alps." In Arno Borst, *Medieval Worlds: Barbarians, Heretics, and Artists in the Middle Ages*, translated by Eric Hansen, 101–22. Chicago: University of Chicago Press, 1992.

Boureau, Alain. *Satan the Heretic: The Birth of Demonology in the Medieval West*. Translated by Teresa Lavender Fagan. Chicago: University of Chicago Press, 2006.

Broedel, Hans Peter. "Fifteenth-Century Witch Beliefs." In *The Oxford Handbook of Witchcraft in Early Modern Europe and Colonial America*, edited by Brian P. Levack, 32–49. Oxford: Oxford University Press, 2013.

Chène, Catherine. "Entre discours pastoral et réflexion démonologique: Le cas du livre V du *Formicarius* de Jean Nider O. P. (ca. 1380–1438)." In *Penser avec les démons: Démonologues et démonologies (XIIIᵉ–XVIIᵉ siècles)*, edited by Martine Ostorero and Julien Véronèse, 57–79. Micrologus' Library 71. Florence: SISMEL, 2015.

Chène, Catherine, and Martine Ostorero. "Démonologie et misogynie: L'émergence d'un discours spécifique sur les femmes dans l'élaboration doctrinale du sabbat au XVᵉ siècle." In *Les femmes dans la société européenne / die Frauen in der europäischen Gesellschaft: 8ᵉ Congrès des Historiennes suisses / 8. Schweizerische Historikerinnentagung*, edited by Anne-Lisa Head-König and Liliane Mottu-Weber, 171–96. Geneva: Droz, 2000.

Ginzburg, Carlo. *Ecstasies: Deciphering the Witches' Sabbath*. Translated by Raymond Rosenthal. New York: Penguin, 1991.

Hansen, Joseph. *Quellen und Untersuchungen zur Geschichte des Hexenwahns und der Hexenverfolgung im Mittelalter*. 1901; repr., Hildesheim: Georg Olms, 1963.

Herzig, Tamar. "Bridging North and South: Inquisitorial Networks and Witchcraft Theory on the Eve of the Reformation." *Journal of Early Modern History* 12 (2008): 361–82.

———. "Flies, Heretics, and the Gendering of Witchcraft." *Magic, Ritual, and Witchcraft* 5 (2010): 51–80.

Kieckhefer, Richard. "Avenging the Blood of Children: Anxiety over Child Victims and the Origins of the European Witch Trials." In *The Devil, Heresy and Witchcraft in the Middle Ages: Essays in Honor of Jeffrey B. Russell*, edited by Alberto Ferreiro, 91–109. Cultures, Beliefs, and Traditions 6. Leiden: Brill, 1998.

———. *European Witch Trials: Their Foundations in Popular and Learned Culture, 1300–1500*. Berkeley: University of California Press, 1976.

———. "The First Wave of Trials for Diabolical Witchcraft." In *The Oxford Handbook of Witchcraft in Early Modern Europe and Colonial America*, edited by Brian P. Levack, 159–78. Oxford: Oxford University Press, 2013.

———. *Magic in the Middle Ages*. Cambridge: Cambridge University Press, 1989.

———. "Mythologies of Witchcraft in the Fifteenth Century." *Magic, Ritual, and Witchcraft* 1 (2006): 79–108.

———. "Witchcraft, Necromancy and Sorcery as Heresy." In *Chasse aux sorcières et démonologie: Entre discours et pratiques (XIVᵉ–XVIIᵉ siècles)*, edited by Martine Ostorero, Georg Modestin, and Kathrin Utz Tremp, 133–53. Micrologus' Library 36. Florence: SISMEL, 2010.

Klaniczay, Gábor. "The Process of Trance: Heavenly and Diabolic Apparitions in Johannes Nider's *Formicarius*." In *Procession, Performance, Liturgy, and Ritual: Essays in Honor of Bryan R. Gillingham*, edited by Nancy Van Deusen, 203–58. Ottawa: Institute of Medieval Music, 2007.

Mercier, Franck, and Martine Ostorero. *L'énigme de la Vauderie de Lyon: Enquête sur l'essor de la chasse aux sorcières entre France et Empire (1430–1480)*. Micrologus' Library 72. Florence: SISMEL, 2015.

Modestin, Georg. "Church Reform and Witch-Hunting in the Diocese of Lausanne: The Example of Bishop George of Saluzzo." In *Heresy and the Making of European Culture: Medieval and Early Modern Perspectives*, edited by Andrew P. Roach and James R. Simpson, 403–10. Farnham: Ashgate, 2013.

———. "'Von der hexen, so in Wallis verbrant wurdent': Eine wieder entdeckte Handschrift mit dem Bericht des Chronisten Hans Fründ über eine Hexenverfolgung im Wallis (1428)." *Vallesia* 60 (2005): 399–409.

Ostorero, Martine. *Le diable au sabbat: Littérature démonologique et sorcellerie (1440–1460)*. Micrologus' Library 38. Florence: SISMEL, 2011.

———. "Itinéraire d'un inquisiteur gâté: Ponce Feugeyron, les Juifs et le sabbat des sorciers." *Médiévales* 43 (2002): 103–18.

———. "Witchcraft." In *The Routledge History of Medieval Magic*, edited by Sophie Page and Catherine Rider, 502–22. London: Routledge, 2019.

Ostorero, Martine, Agostino Paravicini Bagliani, and Kathrin Utz Tremp, with Catherine Chène. *L'imaginaire du sabbat: Edition critique des textes les plus anciens (1430 c.–1440 c.)*. Cahiers Lausannoise d'Histoire Médiévale 26. Lausanne: Université de Lausanne, 1999.

Ostorero, Martine, and Kathrin Utz Tremp, with Georg Modestin. *Inquisition et sorcellerie en Suisse romande: Le register Ac 29 des Archives cantonales vaudoises (1438–1528)*. Cahiers Lausannoise d'Histoire Médiévale 41. Lausanne: Université de Lausanne, 2007.

Paravy, Pierrette. "À propos de la genèse médiévale des chasse aux sorcières: Le traité de Claude Tholosan, juge dauphinois (vers 1436)." *Mélanges de l'École Française de Rome* 91 (1979): 333–79.

———. *De la chrétienté romaine à la Réforme en Dauphiné: Évêques fidèles et déviants (vers 1340–vers 1530)*. 2 vols. Rome: École Française de Rome, 1993.

Stephens, Walter. *Demon Lovers: Witchcraft, Sex, and the Crisis of Belief*. Chicago: University of Chicago Press, 2002.

Tschacher, Werner. *Der Formicarius des Johannes Nider von 1437/38: Studien zu den Anfängen der europäischen Hexenverfolgungen im Spätmittelalter*. Aachen: Shaker, 2000.

Utz Tremp, Kathrin. "The Heresy of Witchcraft in Western Switzerland and Dauphiné (Fifteenth Century)." *Magic, Ritual, and Witchcraft* 6 (2011): 1–10.

———. *Von der Häresie zur Hexerei: "Wirkliche" und imaginäre Sekten im Spätmittelalter.* Monumenta Germaniae Historica Schriften 59. Hannover: Hahnsche Buchhandlung, 2008.

———. "Witches' Brooms and Magic Ointments: Twenty Years of Witchcraft Research at the University of Lausanne (1989–2009)." *Magic, Ritual, and Witchcraft* 5 (2010): 173–87.

INDEX